MORE FABULOUS

Also by Larry Carr: FOUR FABULOUS FACES

FACES

The Evolution and Metamorphosis of
Dolores Del Rio
Myrna Loy
Carole Lombard
Bette Davis and
Katharine Hepburn

BY LARRY CARR

DOUBLEDAY & COMPANY, INC., GARDEN CITY, NEW YORK 1979

ACKNOWLEDGMENTS

Deep appreciation and grateful thanks are due a number of friends and acquaintances for invaluable help on this book.

I am particularly indebted to Douglas Whitney for indispensable aid and generous contributions of rare photographs and background material. Similiar gratitude is tendered Paul Trent, Billy Roy, Ben Carbonetta, Ronald Bowers, Hal Richardson, L. Arnold Weissberger, Ron Alexander, Arthur Dodge, Earl Luick, David Chierchetti, Everett Raymond Kinstler, John Springer, John W. M. Phillips and *Movie Star News* for invaluable aid in securing material and photographs important to this project.

I am beholden to Miss Myrna Loy for her abundant assistance, and for pictures from her personal collection. To Miss Dolores Del Rio and Mr. Lewis Riley go warm thanks for their co-operation and contribution of portraits of Miss Del Rio.

My gratitude to Paul H. Bonner of Condé Nast publications for the use of photographs from *Vanity Fair* magazine. I am immensely grateful to Maureen Myers, Eve Bayne and Annelen Hughes, David Ragen, Jean Bennett, Marjorie Arnold, Jeanne Avery, Barbara Lea and Joan Holode for their time and help.

Recognition and thanks go to Warner Bros., M-G-M, Paramount, RKO, 20th Century-Fox, Columbia and United Artists studios for their help, and to the superb photography of George Hurrell, Clarence S. Bull, Eugene R. Richee, Russell Ball, Preston Duncan, Elmer Fryer, Ray Jones, Ernest A. Bachrach, Otto Dyar, Bert Six and Florence Vandamn. Their cameras so succinctly and successfully captured the glamour, perfection and luxury incarnate of a Hollywood that once was but now exists only on film and in photographs such as theirs.

Special mention must be made of the enormously helpful editorship of Janell Walden; I am deeply thankful for her patience and assistance. And grateful recognition is accorded Laurence Alexander for his strikingly beautiful layouts and design, which make this book such a pleasure to see.

I am indebted to all the above and to any others whom I may have inadvertently overlooked. Without their assistance, I could not have accomplished this book.

August 15, 1977

The author and publisher are grateful to these sources for permission to reproduce the following illustrations:

Condé Nast—page 98; top, page 123; top left, page 227
New York *Post*—top, page 101

DESIGNED BY LAURENCE ALEXANDER

Library of Congress Cataloging in Publication Data
Carr, Larry
More Fabulous Faces
   CONTENTS: Dolores Del Rio.—Myrna Loy.—Carole Lombard.—Bette Davis.—Katharine Hepburn.
   1. Moving-picture actors and actresses—United States—Biography. 2. Moving-picture actors and actresses—United States—Portraits. I. Title.
PN1998.A2C344   791.43′028′0922 [B]
ISBN: 0-385-12819-3
Library of Congress Catalog Card Number 77–16904

CONTENTS

INTRODUCTION

In an age that exalts the commonplace—and a time when taste has succumbed to tawdriness—it's refreshing to peer back at an oh, so recent past when Hollywood was bringing that overworked "glamour" to theaters all over the world, and every week of the year the screen was showing the most beautiful, fabulous faces ever seen at one time in the history of mankind.

This book is a tribute to the beauty and glamour, talent and enduring appeal of five Fabulous Faces from that era: *Dolores Del Rio, Myrna Loy, Carole Lombard, Bette Davis* and *Katharine Hepburn.* All are Star-faces who remain lasting symbols of a glamorous past when Hollywood was at its peak as trend-setter for the entire world and movie stars were Movie Stars!

It is written in admiration . . . but not reverence . . . or awe.

A sequel to *Four Fabulous Faces* (Swanson, Garbo, Crawford and Dietrich), it is devoted to the same photographic demonstration of the evolution and metamorphosis of these five acknowledged Hollywood beauties of the 30's. Chronologically, it traces their gradual transformation from unknown, sometimes undistinguished young women into dazzling Superstars, illustrating the almost unbelievable changes in physiognomy and character undergone by all of them. It is a study in depth of five women who had long periods of great creativity (as well as those disturbing dry spells), whose faces, ability and appeal have endured for nearly fifty years and who still retain that rare aura of star magic.

More Fabulous Faces is the title of this book. It is not *More Beautiful Faces* although all five undoubtedly *are* beautiful to their respective admirers. But then, so are hundreds of other "beautiful" women of the screen, and certainly the movies have had some extraordinary faces during their remarkable history.

The dictionaries define "fabulous" as "incredible, legendary, amazing," "marvelous, astounding," "mythical" and "unbelievable," and one can make a selection of any of these. But nowhere is "fabulous" defined as "beautiful," and beauty was not the criterion for my choices, for beauty per se is too limiting.

What interests me in a face is variety, growth, character and continuation. The camera loves faces with fine bone structure, faces with myriad looks capable of expressing a variety of moods and thoughts, faces that continue to interest and absorb, page after page, over a long period of time.

Where the human face is concerned, it is a mysterious chemistry that determines our responses to a person and her portraits. And though it is through the eye of the photographer that we come into contact with the subject, still it is our own perceptions and attitudes that ultimately color our response. We read things into a face that may or may not be there, seeing it from a personal and individual viewpoint. Today, it sometimes seems easier to distinguish the real from the illusory, the enduring from the transitory, the significant from the trivial.

The choice of these five subjects was achieved only after looking at literally thousands of photographs of faces that once lit up the screen. Some had beauty that lasted for just a short time. Others were photographed only from certain angles and thus had a tiring sameness. The truly Great Faces were those that endured but changed with the times, possessing a variety of looks, moods and expressions. The five faces presented here are unique, and each is a striking contrast to the other four. All are Fabulous Faces.

In the last decade the nostalgia craze, and with it the resurgence of interest in Hollywood and its outstanding personalities, has resulted in a striking knowledge on the part of young people about the movies and stars of earlier decades. Television, film festivals and college courses in cinema history have made film buffs of people of every age—from those who remember these movies from the first time around to a younger public that is just discovering them. All respond to an enchantment, authority and sense of style quite different from the films of today in which only men are contemporary stars and box office attractions.

Gone is the magic of those gorgeous, beautiful women whose films thrilled audiences all over the world. Now, ephemeral women "stars" come and go with disturbing rapidity, lighting the screen for a short time, then fading back into relative dimness. Because of a lack of follow-up roles, the phenomenon of premature stardom too often is followed by comparative obscurity so that last year's "sensation" becomes this year's "who?" This deterioration of women stars is deplorable, their decline depressing.

The role of women on the screen in recent years has become so scaled down that they often seem one-dimensional, particularly when one recalls the larger-than-life characters Hollywood once gave us. There were the great women's films like *Stella Dallas, Mildred Pierce, Zaza, Jezebel, Rain, Madame X, Anna Christie, Anna Karenina, The Trespasser, The Old Maid, Madame Bovary, A Woman's Face* and *Dark Victory*. Today, women who want to identify with a screen counterpart must look to TV soap operas and situation comedies like "Rhoda," "Maude," "Phyllis" and "The Mary Tyler Moore Show" because they no longer exist on the screen. Both the stars and the stories have vanished.

Where are the updated dramatic actresses to match Hepburn, Davis, Garbo, Swanson or Crawford? Is Faye Dunaway our contemporary Davis? Is Jane Fonda today's Hepburn? Is Goldie Hawn the new Lombard?

Certainly, there currently are no young performers who seem capable of giving the buoyant, subtle comedy performance of a Myrna Loy, Carole Lombard, Irene Dunne, Jean Arthur or Claudette Colbert, even were such roles to be written. A Lombard gave free rein to her own irrepressible personality, and her fans felt a magical rapport with her whether she was serious or clowning. And Myrna Loy, with her deceptively casual manner and subtle underplaying, distinguished herself with some of the most adroit comedy ever seen on the screen. Yet she was equally adept at drama. Audiences viewed her with such genuine affection that they crowned her "Queen of the Movies" in 1938 (Gable was "King"), and put her in the box office "Top Ten" for several years.

Beauty is often hampering for an actress. And when her producers and directors, even she, herself, permit too much attention to be focused on that beauty and not on her development as an actress, her opportunities become limited and her career can suffer.

Almost from the inception of her career, Dolores Del Rio's beauty was to prove a mixed blessing. It often so overshadowed her ability that rarely was she given roles commensurate with her talent. Particularly

does this seem true of her career after the advent of talking pictures. In silents, she had been a *star* of such dramatic hits as *Ramona, Resurrection* and *Evangeline,* but in talkies her exotic personality and accent were used mostly to decorate enjoyable but hardly memorable films like *The Bird of Paradise, Flying Down to Rio, Wonder Bar* and *Madame Du Barry.* Finally, she had to return to her native Mexico to re-establish herself as a serious actress. In doing so, she became her country's top star. Interestingly enough, one of her Mexican films, *La Otra (The Other One),* 1947, was remade by Bette Davis as *Dead Ringer* in 1964. With roles in which she was able to exercise her acting skill, roles never given her in Hollywood, Del Rio won four Ariels, the Mexican equivalent of Hollywood's Oscar.

Both Bette Davis and Katharine Hepburn have been termed "First Lady of the Screen," and both have been nominated for the Academy Award more often than any other female performers. In the majority of the films and plays during their long careers they concentrated on drama, although they were seen in occasional comedies: Davis in *It's Love I'm After, The Bride Came C.O.D.* and *The Man Who Came to Dinner;* Hepburn in *Alice Adams, Bringing Up Baby* and *Pat and Mike.* Their films have been fully examined in other books, so this one will not dwell on that aspect of their contributions.

Recently, while discussing the achievements of her Hollywood predecessors, Glenda Jackson said:

"Think of what they had to do, those people in the Golden Age of Hollywood . . . Dietrich, Joan Crawford, for example, and Bette Davis. When you think of the arrant rubbish they transformed, not just into something acceptable but even into something you believed, then you have to acknowledge that their abilities were absolutely incredible—really incredible. Their utilization of the technical means in that way was more than a talent. The fact that Dietrich could come on the set, look at the lights and say, 'No, you're not ready for me!' is almost a stroke of genius."

The gorgeously unique faces of past decades have been succeeded by such a pattern of ordinary ones that it is difficult to compile any comparable list of truly contemporary "beauties." One recalls with awe the range and heterogeneous choice of women once seen on the screen. In the 20's, in addition to the great stars like Pickford, Gish, Swanson, Negri, Norma Talmadge, Pearl White, Mae Murray, Colleen Moore,

Marion Davies, Clara Bow and Garbo, there were such varied beauties as Mary Astor, Vilma Banky, Betty Bronson, Madge Bellamy, Louise Brooks, Eleanor Boardman, Mary Brian, Baclanova, Betty Compson, Sue Carol, Nancy Carroll, Bebe Daniels, Billie Dove, Lily Damita, Corinne Griffith, Janet Gaynor, Phyllis Haver, Jetta Goudal, Lya de Putti, Barbara LaMarr, Dorothy Mackaill, Greta Nissen, Aileen Pringle, Constance Talmadge, Estelle Taylor, Blanche Sweet and Alice White.

From that decade, such fabulous faces as Joan Crawford, Myrna Loy, Carole Lombard, Jean Arthur, Norma Shearer, Dolores Del Rio and Gloria Swanson continued into the 30's to join Constance and Joan Bennett, Adrienne Ames, Joan Blondell, Claudette Colbert, Ruth Chatterton, Madeleine Carroll, Bette Davis, Marlene Dietrich, Madge Evans, Kay Francis, Alice Faye, Jean Harlow, Katharine Hepburn, Ann Harding, Lillian Harvey, Miriam Hopkins, Ruby Keeler, Hedy Lamarr, Jeanette MacDonald, Merle Oberon, Ginger Rogers, Roz Russell, Anna Sten, Barbara Stanwyck, Sylvia Sidney, Ann Sothern, Helen Twelvetrees, Lupe Velez, Fay Wray, Mae West and Loretta Young. Most of them were highly individual, and their looks, acting and personalities were groomed and developed to accentuate this quality.

Considering this prodigious number of stars once seen on screens all over the world, it's interesting to consider the talents who survived. Some burned out prematurely, many lost themselves to narcissism, and self-destruction overtook others. Mary Pickford, Garbo, Norma Shearer and Irene Dunne retired completely while Janet Gaynor, Ruby Keeler, Loretta Young, Mae West and Jean Arthur made occasional "returns." Some have never stopped performing: Lillian Gish, Gloria Swanson, Davis, Dietrich, Colbert, Del Rio, Loy, Ginger Rogers and Barbara Stanwyck have all remained prominent figures long after most of their contemporaries disappeared from the theatrical scene. And only death could halt the performing drive of the late Joan Crawford, Rosalind Russell and Constance Bennett.

Certainly glamour was one of Hollywood's most precious commodities in its golden days. One dictionary describes it as "alluring charm or fascination often based on illusion," while another says, "a deceptive or enticing charm." But Hollywood defined it as what it took to transform an actress into a Great Screen Personality. Ever since the first camera crank turned on the sunlit charms of some heavy-lidded silent siren, glamour was imposed on those who didn't have it and idealized even further on those who did. The purveyors who distilled its heady essence had to keep the public dazzled.

It was the age of utter perfection. The intimate scrutiny of the camera closeup demanded that nothing mar that perfection, or the illusion of it. The face must show no lines, wrinkles or blemishes of any kind. The teeth had to be faultless, every hair was in place (even when the actress was sleeping—or ill—or dying) and every piece of apparel was impeccable and unwrinkled. The deep and far-ranging changes wrought by the Hollywood makeup and fashion artists not only incredibly transformed the appearances of these actresses but often brought key changes in their personalities. As they acquired beauty, wealth and worldwide fame, they also developed style, poise, assurance and authority so that, as this book illustrates, early photographs are astonishingly different from the ultimate star-images that captured the imagination of the world. The "star system," then at its height, consisted of the subordination of everything else to the supreme importance of that star: story plots, clothes, sets, music, even the directors and writers (who now dominate the industry) were then built around those gods and goddesses of the screen.

Hollywood created a universal concept of beauty and its women reflected the ideals and desires of each decade. Fashions varied and styles changed—sweet to sophisticated, voluptuous to slender, long hair to short, then back to long. But no matter what the look, the end result had to be perfection so that the illusion of youth and consummate beauty was nurtured to its utmost.

One of the screen's essential accomplishments is its preservation of the past. Through the special magic of the movies, not only are the great performances of yesterday maintained for future generations but the youth and beauty of the performances themselves are kept intact. It's unfortunate that life cannot imitate art for, whereas in real life we must watch our friends and ourselves grow older, on the screen our favorite actors and actresses never change. They remain exactly as we remembered them—forever young, and preserved with immortality. Time and again, dazzled and intrigued, we can watch them and find them always the same . . . never older but "as lovely as ever."

Photographs, too, have this ability to preserve the past so that other generations can study and savor the look of an era . . . the quality of a person . . . the timelessness of a face. A picture compilation such as

this book offers the opportunity for repeated viewings and analyses, thus enabling the beholder to enjoy or probe, at will.

Carole Lombard died too young to encounter the problem of encroaching maturity, but the others illustrated here met the passing years gracefully with intelligence and dignity. Hepburn beautifully etched the ripeness of feminine middle age in *The Rainmaker*, *Summertime* and *The African Queen*. Davis, who played roles much older than her own age in *The Old Maid*, *The Corn Is Green* and *The Little Foxes* as well as her brilliant Elizabeth I, thus was able to mature gracefully on the screen in *All About Eve* and *The Star:* logical preparations for the character roles she plays today.

Loy and Del Rio went with equal ease into older roles: Loy with *The Best Years of Our Lives* and *The Red Pony* into character and mother roles (the recent *The Women* on Broadway and her touring vehicle, *Barefoot in the Park*). Del Rio played Sal Mineo's mother in *Cheyenne Autumn*, Elvis Presley's mother in *Flaming Star,* and more recently, Omar Sharif's mother in *More Than a Miracle*. The personal maturity of both women has matched that of their screen roles.

All five stars have a place in screen history that is secure and unique, for each has made her own special contribution: a different look, a special personality, an acting style completely her own that was developed by hard work, trial and error and a total devotion to her art and self. No two were alike in looks or style and each is a striking contrast to the other. A Garbo, Hepburn, Davis, Loy, Crawford or Del Rio didn't just happen; that lasting place in screen annals was achieved by drive and discipline. And we must not forget the constant exposure given them by their studios: during their peak years one could see them in three or four films a year, which developed a steady and loyal following for them.

Also at that time, movie magazines, totally different from such periodicals today, were edited and written by bright, knowledgeable young people who were devoted to the movies and filled with affectionate enthusiasm for the screen and its artists . . . performers, directors, writers, designers, et al. These magazines were a vital force in acquainting the public with stars on their way to fame, and in keeping movie fans interested when their careers began to wane. Fans felt that they knew the stars personally, so their affection was deep and devoted. They went to watch the star, not necessarily the film: "Let's go see the new Hepburn (or whoever) picture," they said; and if, as did happen, the film was weak or poor, it was soon followed by another one that preserved their loyalty and interest.

So here is my tribute to five cinema legends who pioneered new aspects of screen performing, persevering with dedication to build lasting and illustrious careers. In myriad ways they all have made a contribution to our lives and culture and have exerted a notable influence upon women the world over.

All are unique.
All are legendary performers.
And certainly all are Fabulous Faces!

MORE FABULOUS FACES

DOLORES DEL RIO

The era of the Silent Screen, during which a young and totally inexperienced Dolores Del Rio came to Hollywood, is much too rich and complex a period to be condensed into a few pages or even one book. But a brief look back to circa 1925 is sketched here in order to illustrate and explain the very different Hollywood to which she came. It was a time when the screen was importing talent from every part of the world, and film hopefuls of every age and description arrived daily seeking careers. Especially attracted to the new Mecca were thousands of pretty young girls seeking fame and fortune.

It was in 1925 that the Hollywood careers of five of the screen's Superstars began. They were Dolores Del Rio from Mexico; Myrna Loy from Montana; Carole Lombard from Indiana; Greta Garbo from Sweden; and Joan Crawford from Texas. The screen lives of three of them—Del Rio, Loy and Crawford—were to last for over fifty years!

They all arrived in the screen capital at a significant time in the history of the movies: the Silent Screen was at its very apex. Every week, theaters all over the world were showing probably the greatest talents ever assembled in one town. The term "superstar" was not in use then, but Hollywood and the world knew what a Star was. Already the screen had produced an astonishing number of actors and actresses who were just that—names that would become legendary in any catalogue of all-time screen greats: Chaplin, Pickford, Fairbanks, Lillian Gish, Valentino, Swanson, Tom Mix, William S. Hart, Lon Chaney, Constance and Norma Talmadge, Harold Lloyd, Mae Murray, Buster Keaton, Nazimova, Pola Negri and Clara Bow. It was a formidable congregation of talent.

In just a few, brief years from their crude, embryonic beginning, the movies had witnessed the maturing of such diverse directorial talents as D. W. Griffith, Cecil B. DeMille, Erich Von Stroheim, Rex Ingram, Henry King, Clarence Brown, Allan Dwan, Marshall Neilan, James Cruze and many others. The director was supreme in silent films, for he also functioned as producer. In addition, there were the designers, writers, costume people, cameramen and technicians of every description.

The Silent Screen was unique in the history of entertainment: for the very first time, a universal form of amusement had been created, one capable of reaching audiences in the most remote spots of the globe. As Gloria Swanson recalled, "They put us in cans, like sardines, and shipped us all over the world." And "going to the movies" was then so inexpensive that it quickly became a weekly event for the whole family.

In a remarkably short time, screen acting evolved a style all its own. Pantomime was developed to its highest art form, affecting the whole spectrum of performing. Expressing thought as well as emotion through the least possible means (a slight gesture, a suggested smile, a glance of the eye or lift of the eyebrow) conveyed meanings with an ease and subtlety impossible in the previously exaggerated and necessarily broader style of the stage. Many years later, when he returned to the stage after making his early Hollywood films, Laurence Olivier was to say that he felt the need to tone down his performance.

In silent films, a further simplicity and artlessness became possible with the advancing use of the closeup. Its intimacy enabled audiences to perceive the actor's every thought and emotion. They responded by becoming creative contributors—supplying sound, voice and dialogue to the imaginative visuals on the screen.

It is not surprising that, with few exceptions, the best Silent Screen actors were those with little or no stage experience, for they had nothing to unlearn. Valentino, Chaney, Swanson, Colleen Moore, Harold Lloyd and Clara Bow, for example, all were screen products. Others, like Pickford, Gish, Chaplin, Fairbanks and Keaton, had had only a slight acquaintance with the stage. By the mid-20's, inexpe-

1

rienced young women like Del Rio, Janet Gaynor, Myrna Loy, Carole Lombard and Joan Crawford were being put under contract and groomed for stardom. Many fell by the wayside, but a surprising number developed into big stars.

At the time Del Rio came to Hollywood, most of the top female stars had husbands who participated in their careers as producers or directors, helping to fight their battles while protecting and guiding them. Prominent were the combinations of Pickford and Fairbanks, Norma Talmadge and Joseph Schenck, Maria Corda and Alexander Korda, Colleen Moore and John McCormick, Corinne Griffith and Walter Morosco, Florence and King Vidor, Mae Murray and Robert Z. Leonard and the team of Marion Davies and W. R. Hearst. In a short time, Norma Shearer and Irving Thalberg joined this group. Gloria Swanson and Pola Negri fought on alone and Del Rio was to do likewise although, during her first few years, director Edwin Carewe was her guide and mentor.

Del Rio came into pictures at a time of unprecedented change and development in the film industry. Some of the smaller, independent companies were finding it expedient to join forces with larger studios and already under way by 1925 were consolidations which portended the big studios of the 30's. Before this time, for the most part, Hollywood had been a town of loosely knit studios built around star personalities such as Harold Lloyd, Chaplin, Keaton, Fairbanks, Marion Davies, Mary Pickford, and such producer-directors as Griffith, DeMille, Hal Roach and Mack Sennett. The larger studios were Famous Players, Fox, Biograph, Universal, Goldwyn, First National, Selznick and Metro. Most of the smaller companies, not yet absorbed by the larger ones, were still releasing their own films. But this was beginning to change by 1925.

In 1924, when the Metro studio consolidated with Goldwyn to become Metro-Goldwyn, under contract were Mae Murray, Norma Shearer, John Gilbert, Ramon Novarro, Aileen Pringle, Conrad Nagel and Mae Busch. L. B. Mayer was appointed chief of production, assisted by Irving Thalberg, who moved over from Universal studios. In 1925 the studio became Metro-Goldwyn-Mayer, signed contracts with Lillian Gish, William Haines, Buster Keaton, Lon Chaney, Marion Davies and Jackie Coogan, and started billing itself as the studio with "More Stars Than There Are in Heaven."

Famous Players had joined forces with Jesse Lasky and was briefly known as Famous Players-Lasky, featuring such stars as Swanson, Negri, Rod La Rocque, Bebe Daniels, Richard Dix and Lois Wilson. When Cecil B. DeMille left to form his own studio, the B. P. Schulberg organization was absorbed. This final combination became Paramount Studios.

Warner Bros., with only a handful of stars, bought First National and acquired Loretta Young, Richard Barthelmess and Dorothy Mackaill, among others.

Fairbanks, Pickford, Chaplin and D. W. Griffith formed United Artists, released their own productions and, later, those of Gloria Swanson, Samuel Goldwyn, and ultimately five Del Rio films, the Edwin Carewe productions of *Resurrection, Ramona, Revenge, Evangeline* and *The Bad One.*

Some of the finest silent pictures ever made (many of which are still being shown) were released in 1925: *He Who Gets Slapped, The Merry Widow, Greed, The Big Parade* and *The Unholy Three* from M-G-M; *Peter Pan, The Vanishing American, Madame Sans Gene* and *Forbidden Paradise* from Paramount; *Quo Vadis* and *The Last Laugh* imported from Europe; Chaplin's *The Gold Rush;* Fairbanks' *Don Q;* Sam Goldwyn's *Stella Dallas* and *The Dark Angel;* Harold Lloyd's *The Freshman;* Lon Chaney's *The Phantom of the Opera;* Colleen Moore's *So Big;* Valentino's *The Eagle;* and Lubitsch's *Lady Windermere's Fan.*

In just two years, with the birth of sound in 1927, the death knell would be sounded for the glories of the Silent Screen, and only in museum showings and revivals would this art form survive. In the past few decades a growing appreciation for the extraordinary skill and unique charm of the Silent Screen has been reawakened, and overdue recognition given its stars and films.

The American idea of beauty in 1925 was typified by the choices of five hundred newspaper critics and columnists for "The Ten Most Beautiful Women on the Screen." For the most part, their selections reflect the then prevalent penchant for pastel prettiness as the criterion for beauty: Mary Astor, May Allison, Marion Davies, Corinne Griffith, Mae Murray, Alice Terry and Florence Vidor. The three exceptions were Gloria Swanson, Norma Shearer and Pola Negri. Interestingly enough, except for Davies, Murray and Vidor, all of these women are still alive today, over fifty years later. A similar list made in 1929 included Del Rio, Billie Dove, Vilma Banky and Dolores Costello. Prettiness was still a factor but judges were beginning to acquire an understanding of and appreciation for bone structure and the sculptured face with planes and character.

In the 20's and 30's it was thought that blondes usually photographed best; they were "preferred" not only by gentlemen but by the camera. The majority of screen imports were blondes—or soon became so— as exemplified by Garbo, Banky, Dietrich, Anna Sten, Tala Birell, Gwili Andre, Isa Miranda, Maria Corda, Greta Nissen and Ingrid Bergman.

Brown-haired beauties, who came next in the cameramen's preferences, included Norma Talmadge, Swanson, Shearer, Irene Dunne, Crawford, Loretta

Young and Fay Wray. Among redheads, whose hair photographed dark, were Myrna Loy, Janet Gaynor, Clara Bow, Mary Astor and Katharine Hepburn.

Only a few brunettes achieved stardom in the 20's. Theda Bara, Pola Negri and Barbara LaMarr were three exceptions when Del Rio joined the group. Nita Naldi, Louise Brooks, Lya de Putti, Lil Dagover, Armida from Mexico and Conchita Montenegro from Spain, Kay Francis, Merle Oberon, Hedy Lamarr and Lupe Velez were later to swell the ranks of brunettes but, even among these, there were few genuine types with olive skin and black eyes. A Del Rio was very rare.

When Dolores Del Rio first arrived in Hollywood, her mentor, director Carewe, placed her under contract to First National studios where the female stars were Colleen Moore, Corinne Griffith, Constance and Norma Talmadge, and Barbara LaMarr. The Misses LaMarr and Griffith were considered two of the movies' genuine beauties and First National soon added another, the exquisite Billie Dove. Since nearly all these women had husbands who were producers or directors, the competition for scripts was terrific. Evidently Carewe thought so because in 1926 he lent Del Rio to Fox for *What Price Glory,* her first important picture. The favorable reception she received led to a contract with that studio, where she filmed *The Loves of Carmen, The Gateway to the Moon, No Other Women* and *The Red Dance.*

Like Myrna Loy and Carole Lombard, Del Rio's love of dance and experience in that field had given her an ease of movement and an ability to express emotion through movement that was ideal for the required pantomime of silent pictures. So she was readily able to learn the screen technique and by 1928 had become an important film star.

Lolita Dolores Asúnsolo de Martinez was born on August 3, 1905, in Durango, Mexico, the only child of Antonia Lopez Negrete de Asúnsolo and Jesús L. Asúnsolo. Her father, from a prominent Spanish-Basque family in Chihuahua, was the director of the Bank of Durango; her mother was descended from the Toltecs.

In 1910 the family fled to Mexico City to escape Pancho Villa, who seized their home and her father's bank in Durango. When Dolores was six she was enrolled in the Convent of St. Joseph in Mexico City, which was run by French nuns. From early childhood she "adored dancing" and, since young ladies were expected to have "accomplishments," at seven she began taking lessons from Felipa Lopez, a prominent dancer. It was her dancing that later attracted the eye of a Hollywood director and led to her career in films.

Early in 1921, shortly after her fifteenth birthday, she was married to Jaime Martinez del Rio, a socially prominent lawyer who had been educated in England and France. Señor del Rio, eighteen years her senior, took her on an extended honeymoon with long stays in Madrid, Paris, Rome and London. While in Madrid in 1922, she danced at a social function for the wounded of the Melilla campaign during the Spanish-Moroccan War and, that same year, was presented to the King and Queen of Spain.

After the couple's return to Mexico City, Dolores was encouraged by her husband to continue her dancing so she prepared "intimate ballets" which she choreographed. "It was my only emotional escape. With my dancing, I realized that I wanted also to act," she later recalled. Her husband was interested in writing and introduced his wife to literature, archaeology and classical music. "Jaime taught me to cultivate the spirit and opened my young eyes to a new world."

With mother at five, and in painting at twelve

In wedding gown at fifteen

In 1925, a close friend, painter Adolfo Best Maugard, brought two American couples from Hollywood, honeymooners Edwin Carewe and Mary Aiken and film stars Claire Windsor and Bert Lytell, to the del Rio home for tea one afternoon. As entertainment for her guests, young Señora del Rio danced the tango and made a decided impression on director Carewe. "He called my husband over and said, 'Your wife should come to Hollywood with us and go into the movies.' . . . After that, we saw Mr. Carewe many times and always he offers me a contract. Finally, I decided to accept." The decision was not easy. Her own family was reluctant for her to go and her husband's family disapproved completely. It was pointed out to her that a lady of good family in Mexico did not become an actress; it just was not done! But she was eager to try her luck and replied, "Very well, I will be the first." And the first she was.

Her husband concurred with her wish, and later she was to say that his encouragement came from the wish for a total change in both their lives. "Jaime was eager to escape a social setting that did not satisfy his restlessness, and hoped to develop his literary inclinations by writing scripts in Hollywood."

The couple left Mexico and arrived in the film capital on August 27, 1925.

Beauty has no boundaries!

Probably the greatest evidence for this statement is the scope of world-wide beauty that emerged in Hollywood during the 20's and 30's. Glittering and gorgeous women of every nationality, description and coloring—from the palest blonde to the deepest brunette—graced the screen during those decades.

It all began in 1923. Imported from Germany that year was the international Polish star, sultry Pola Negri, whose exotic beauty and tempestuous behavior shook Hollywood to its rafters. She soon rivaled Gloria Swanson in popularity and, because of her success, there began the aptly termed "Foreign Invasion." Actors and actresses, directors and writers from every part of the globe poured into Hollywood for a try at the Silent Screen. Some of them were brought over by the studios in the hope of finding another Negri, another Valentino, another Lubitsch. Others just came on their own.

By 1925 the "invasion" was at its height. From south of the border in Mexico came Del Rio, Lupe Velez, Raquel Torres and Armida; Greta Garbo arrived from Sweden, Vilma Banky and Maria Corda from Hungary, Greta Nissen from Norway. From France came Arlette Marchal, Jetta Goudal and Lili Damita; from Russia Olga Baclanova; from Germany Lya de Putti, Camilla Horn and Lil Dagover.

When talkies arrived, at first there was concern that foreign accents would prove unacceptable to American audiences and a problem for the overseas market.

The studios hastily dropped some of the biggest foreign names: Negri, Emil Jannings, Vilma Banky. But the successful talkie debut of Garbo followed by the extraordinary popularity of Marlene Dietrich proved the fallacy of that theory, and another Foreign Invasion began. To Hollywood came Anna Sten, Elissa Landi, Lillian Harvey, Gwili Andre, Tala Birell, Lil Dagover (again), Sari Maritza and, later, Hedy Lamarr, Ilona Massey, Merle Oberon, Maria Montez, Dorothea Wieck and Isa Miranda. Hollywood was really the first United Nations!

Of all the beautiful imports who came to Hollywood in the 20's and 30's and brought such diversity of loveliness to the movies, only Dolores Del Rio is still performing on the screen. Her career, which has persisted over fifty years, remains one of the most enduring in film history.

The del Rios (left) and director Edwin Carewe

The young Mexican matron of twenty who came to Hollywood to try her luck in films bore little resemblance to the acknowledged beauty of world-wide fame she was to become in a few short years. Shy and reserved, she dressed conservatively and wore almost no makeup. The film colony found her "interesting" and "pretty in a foreign way," but privately some thought her "kinda dowdy" and "too sedate." The consensus was that other exotics like Pola Negri, Nita Naldi and Barbara LaMarr had little to fear!

Her producer and mentor, Edwin Carewe, decided a publicity campaign was in order and Harry Wilson, a top publicist, was given the assignment. With her promising appearance and social background, a resourceful press agent might do wonders. Wilson did.

A 1925 portrait of Mrs. Jaime del Rio, taken in Mexico City shortly before her departure for Hollywood.

Del Rio's convent education, her marriage at fifteen, her European travels and social triumphs, her presentation to the King and Queen of Spain, plus her jewels, gowns and personal distinction were all readily adaptable to colorful exploitation. Before she finished her second film Wilson had made her a well-known personality as newspapers and magazines flashed picture after picture and story after story. The photograph shown on the following page is an example: the studio caption says, "Dolores Del Rio has placed the photos of her screen idols on her comb but has left the center space for the Great Unknown." By coincidence, all the idols—Ben Lyon, Lloyd Hughes, Lewis Stone, Milton Sills, Ronald Colman and Richard Barthelmess—were under contract to her studio, First National (see next page).

Peggy Hamilton, a contemporary fashion expert and designer who earlier had made clothes for Gloria Swanson, took Del Rio under her wing and together they created a wardrobe that established the young starlet as one of "Hollywood's Best Dressed Women." Peggy also gave exquisite parties where fan writers and the press met the blooming novice and found her as dazzling in appearance as she was gracious in manner. Within a year, Del Rio had been selected as a WAMPAS Baby Star and was playing leads in important films.

Dolores Del Rio, movie hopeful, a brief time later. (For screen purposes, the small *d* in del Rio was capitalized.)

THE WAMPAS BABY STARS OF 1926

In 1922, members of the Western Association of Motion Picture Advertisers conceived an idea to promote talented and attractive young screen hopefuls and, at the same time, enhance the prestige of the press agents in the picture industry. Each year they would pick "those who during the past year have shown the most talent and promise for eventual stardom." WAMPAS was the acronym devised from the name of the organization. The studios, realizing how useful the idea could be, backed the concept, which attracted widespread interest and attention from both the public and the press.

The selectees were chosen in January of each year and, after national publicity and extensive attention, were then "presented" at a large ball a short time later. During the twelve years of its existence, WAMPAS made some very astute choices, picking such future greats as Colleen Moore, Clara Bow, Lois Wilson, Laura La Plante, Evelyn Brent, Lupe Velez, Jean Arthur, Loretta Young, Joan Blondell and Ginger Rogers.

But the choice for 1926 was outstanding. No other year produced such an impressive collection of future Stars.

Top row, left to right: Mary Astor, Dolores Costello, Fay Wray, Marceline Day and Mary Brian. *Middle row:* Janet Gaynor, Sally O'Neil, Vera Reynolds and Edna Marian. *Bottom row:* Joan Crawford, Dolores Del Rio, Joyce Compton and Sally Long.

A considerable change in Dolores Del Rio's appearance and attitude took place in Hollywood. The modest young wife who posed demurely in her garden grew into a poised, self-confident star who faced the camera with assurance and authority by 1931.

After small parts in four films in which she learned ease before the camera, her first real break came when she played the role of Charmaine in *What Price Glory,* one of the most highly praised and successful pictures of 1926. The next year, her career continued to progress with her acclaimed performance in Tolstoy's *Resurrection,* in which Del Rio made a very favorable impression on the public. Critics, too, were impressed.

The May 1927 issue of *Photoplay* picked Del Rio's *Resurrection* as one of the month's best, declaring, "Director Carewe has built two magnificent sequences, one in which Katuska gives way to the importunities of the passionate Dmitri and, later, when the disheveled and dissolute Katuska faces her accusers in court. Take our word for it, Miss Del Rio rises to genuine heights. Rod La Rocque, too, does admirable work . . . but he is overshadowed by Miss Del Rio's amazing performance."

Mordaunt Hall, in the New York *Times,* September 27, 1927, wrote of *The Loves of Carmen:* "Pola Negri, Geraldine Farrar and Theda Bara each have had their turn before the camera at impersonating the tempestuous wench. Miss Del Rio's characterization is apt to make the Carmens of the past relatively conservative. . . . This new Carmen is fiery beyond question."

Del Rio's advancement as an artist and prominent film star was evidenced by the critics' reviews of her 1928 film *Ramona* and the 1929 *Evangeline.* The August 1928 *Photoplay* picked *Ramona* as one of the "Best Films" of the month, saying ". . . splendid acting by Dolores Del Rio. . . . At the end, when she recovers her memory, her work rises to the heights."

By the time she made *Ramona* with Warner Baxter, her look had already changed greatly from that of the young woman who arrived from Mexico three years earlier.

Of *Evangeline, Screenland,* October 1929, wrote, "Dolores Del Rio, her flaming Latin beauty disguised in the demure cap and costume of the Acadian heroine, gives a moving and graceful performance. Her pleasant voice is heard in several agreeable chansons." Norbert Lusk declared in the November 1929 issue of *Picture Play,* "*Evangeline,* in my opinion, is Del Rio's finest performance since *Resurrection.* It is beautifully sincere and infinitely pathetic. Her singing is haunting, her voice flexible and sweet, and her transformation into a bent, aged sister in the last episode is admirably devoid of histrionics." *Photoplay,* August 1929: "Del Rio, singing both in French and English, gives a fine characterization as the French peasant girl and her transformation as the old lady is striking."

Del Rio figured prominently in the early talkie theme songs, "Charmaine," "Ramona" and "Evangeline"; she recorded "Ramona" for (RCA) Victor in 1929 when the practice of movie stars recording their film hits was at its height. Many of these recordings, by Del Rio, Gloria Swanson, Bebe Daniels, Buddy Rogers, John Boles, Lupe Velez, Pola Negri and Marlene Dietrich, have been reissued in the past few years.

With Don Alvarado in *The Loves of Carmen*

With Warner Baxter in *Ramona*

Seen "at home" in 1926, in 1937, in 1929 and 1935

Portraits from a 1930 camera sitting. Del Rio was not only the first Mexican actress to become a star in Hollywood, but the most enduring. Her contemporaries, Lupe Velez, Rosita Moreno, Conchita Montenegro, Armida, Raquel Torres and others, came and went.

It seems to me, as evidenced here and on other pages, that the Joan Crawford look in the early 30's had its influence on the ultimate appearance of Del Rio. In 1930–31, when Crawford emerged as a vivid camera beauty, women all over the world were copying her style of makeup and dress, and nowhere was her distinctive look more imitated than in Hollywood. Gone were the pretty pastel type of beauty and the rosebud mouth. In their place came the face with planes, the sculptured look. The camera, aided by a change in makeup and different style of lighting, produced a new type of beauty of which Del Rio was a forerunner.

Discarding the soft-focus prettiness of the 20's, she cut her long hair, enlarged the shape of her mouth, altered the style of her eyebrows and emphasized her exquisite bone structure. There emerged the dazzling beauty seen here and in subsequent pictures. Hers became one of the truly Great Faces.

LEADING MEN

Left to right:
Edmund Lowe in *What Price Glory,* 1926
Ralph Forbes in *The Trail of '98,* '28
Joel McCrea in *The Bird of Paradise,* '32
Dick Powell in *Wonder Bar,* '34
Fred Astaire in *Flying Down to Rio,* '33
Douglas Fairbanks, Jr., in *Accused,* '36
John Howard and Wallace Beery in *The Man from Dakota,* '40
Joseph Cotten in *Journey into Fear,* '42
George Sanders in *International Settlement,* '38

Del Rio also played opposite Rod La Rocque, Walter Pidgeon, Victor McLaglen, Don Alvarado, Charles Farrell, Pat O'Brien, Warren William, Richard Dix and Orson Welles in her Hollywood films. Her Mexican movies are described later.

Never was Del Rio's new beauty more evident than in *Madame Du Barry,* 1934, in which she displayed an unsuspected gift for comedy. Unfortunately the film, which was made just prior to the formation of the Legion of Decency, suffered a severe cutting in order to meet the standards of the new censorship. The results were apparent in Norbert Lusk's *Picture Play* review: "A sumptuously beautiful rewrite . . . a feast for the eye but rather lean fare for the mind. The spectator finds entertainment in admiring the beautiful figure that Dolores Del Rio presents. Never has she looked more ravishing nor indulged in more spirited tantrums. It isn't a real character, though, but a lithograph swept by a bold brush."

PARTIES

Of Hollywood's golden days with its fabulous parties, Del Rio recalled, "You can't imagine what it was like; parties that took weeks of planning, the great decorators like Billy Haines who would re-do a house for just a party. Marion Davies once turned her beach house into a circus tent and the guests came dressed as clowns, bareback riders, acrobats, etc. Imagine Marlene Dietrich, Clark Gable, Norma Shearer dressed for a circus party! Marion also gave great parties at San Simeon, that fantastic palace of William Randolph Hearst's.

"They were incredible days . . . like a gorgeous, magnificent movie, with all kinds of people, the Jock Whitneys and Nelson Rockefellers, politicians from Washington, people from Europe. And there were the famous parties at Chaplin's . . . exclusive, small parties for the more intellectual set . . . Somerset Maugham, Noel Coward, John Steinbeck, mad people like Fitzgerald and Hemingway."

When she was married to Cedric Gibbons, M-G-M's top art director, the couple had open-house parties on Sundays in their ultra-modern home at Santa Monica overlooking the sea. Gable and Lombard, Errol Flynn and Lili Damita, Constance Bennett and Gilbert Roland, directors John Ford and King Vidor would drop by for tennis, a swim and buffet dinners. "The Jack Warners gave some of the most wonderful parties; Hollywood had glamour then! But, like the rest of the world, Hollywood has changed enormously. The whole Star system is dead . . . there are no Garbos, no Gables, no Dietrichs. Today, the directors are the stars!"

Opposite page, Dolores with:
Ramon Novarro and Conchita Montenegro (bottom left); Marlene Dietrich and Douglas Fairbanks, Jr. (top); (left to right) Louella Parsons, Janet Gaynor, Gene Raymond and Marion Davies; (left to right) Miriam Hopkins, Merle Oberon and Norma Shearer

Del Rio with two of her former leading men and good friends:

Pat O'Brien in 1937 in *In Caliente* and twenty-five years later

Gilbert Roland and Del Rio at the 1937 preview of *Juarez* (why wasn't she cast as the dark Empress Carlotta instead of Bette Davis?) and again in the late 50's when they were reunited for a TV show, "Mexican Fiesta"

DANCE

Bird of Paradise

Flying Down to Rio with Fred Astaire

Resurrection

Journey into Fear with Jack Durant

Wonder Bar with Ricardo Cortez

In Caliente with Don Carlos

FASHION

Dolores Del Rio was made for fashion extremes and her elegance is international. Her gleaming, seal-black hair, her silky beautiful skin, which has been described as the palest café au lait, and her slim figure and aristocratic bearing made her a designer's dream. Her style evolved from the rich, very Mexican look she brought to Hollywood in the mid-20's. By the early 30's she was wearing clothes that indicated no national origin: the style was high and, on screen or off, Del Rio always dressed like a star.

She recalls, "In the 30's, there were three great movie fashion designers: Adrian, Orry-Kelly and Irene. Kelly [seen here with Del Rio] could handle period fashions as well as contemporary ones. He did my beautiful costumes for *Madame Du Barry*. Adrian was master of the modern while Irene made gentlewomen of all of us. They designed clothes that nobody else had so that women turned to the movies to see exciting and individual clothes. Hollywood set the fashion pace in a way that has never been captured anywhere since.

"The illusive quality that movie stars of the 30's had is not around today. Now, young actresses are devoid of mystery and what was called glamour . . . so different from that magical something which Garbo and Dietrich gave to the public. That air of mystery is more than just beauty . . . it's style . . . it's a great unknown . . . it's elegance. And elegance, like true beauty, comes from within.

"Yes, I love clothes, but always classical. Is it true that the world thinks of me always in black or white? Well, I do prefer them. I belong to the traditional French school of wearing black as the most elegant. . . . White suits me best; it's good for my eyes and my hair."

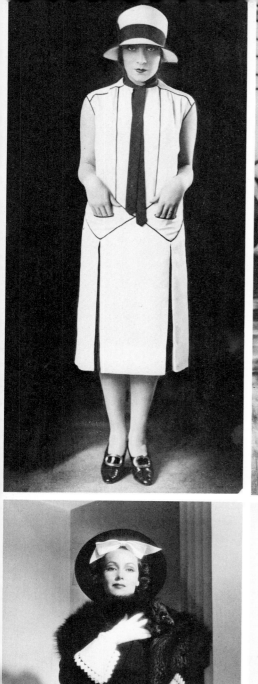

The internationally famed photographer Baron George Hoyningen-Huene, in a discussion of the Great Beauties of Hollywood in *Photoplay*, August 1934, ranked Del Rio second only to Garbo.

"She wears less makeup than any of the stars I have met, yet her vividness is breathtaking. The bone structure of her head and body is magnificent; her skin is like ripe fruit. She has sinuous yet artless grace; her face is so perfectly constructed that she can be photographed in any light, at any angle. Wherever the light falls, it composes beauty. I photographed her in the morning sun, it made no difference. She is the most beautiful Latin since Cavalieri, more lovely than Raquel Meller."

Hats of any size or description were worn with chic and flair. Seen here are portraits from 1935 through 1945.

Before she returned to Mexico to continue her career in 1942, her last Hollywood film was *Journey into Fear*, directed by Orson Welles. After her divorce from Cedric Gibbons, Del Rio and Welles were considered a "romantic item"; they are seen here at a party to raise funds for Britain. (At Welles's left is Herbert Marshall, and on Del Rio's right is Charles Chaplin, who looks as though he's about to spill his dessert.)

Dolores and her parents, Mr. and Mrs. J. L. Asúnsolo

Among Del Rio's good friends were Fay Wray, whom she first met when they were WAMPAS Baby Stars together in 1926, Marlene Dietrich and the frank and outspoken Constance Bennett. The latter sometimes took verbal shots at some of her contemporaries but for Del Rio she had only admiration and warm feelings, saying, "What an extraordinarily progressive person Dolores has been! She came to Hollywood, a strange city in a foreign land, to begin an acting career. She had to learn general customs as well as the technique of the screen, and this was particularly formidable because she didn't speak English.

"I admire her earnestness about her work; nothing is too much trouble! Her screen record to date hasn't come up to her dreams. She is ambitious to be more than just a leading lady; being decorative is not enough, for Dolores is resolved eventually to portray characters of real consequence. The only picture ever to approach her ideal was *Resurrection,* she claims." (*Screenland,* November 1935.)

Like most of the other studios, Warner Bros. seemed to think that her greatest asset was her fabulous beauty. During her sojourn there, she was cast in few noteworthy pictures: *Wonder Bar, Madame DuBarry, In Caliente, I Live for Love,* and *The Widow from Monte Carlo.*

During her seventeen years in Hollywood, Del Rio seldom got roles commensurate with her proven ability. Her silent pictures gave her talent the most scope, but in talkies she rarely got parts that offered opportunities for character probing. Her great beauty was emphasized to the neglect of her dramatic capability. "My Hollywood pictures almost ruined me. I was forced to do glamour parts and I hated it." Like Myrna Loy in her early career, she was usually cast as an exotic, playing a succession of Indian, Russian, French and Polynesian girls. As early as 1929 she was protesting, "It seems that I am always a peasant!" Possibly consoling herself, she continued, "I like to play in old clothes, though. Then I don't have to think of anything but the character; you cannot fling yourself around when you're a lady.

"But someday I would like to play a Mexican woman and show what life in Mexico really is. No one has shown the artistic side—nor the social."

Finally she was compelled to return to Mexico to achieve proper recognition as an actress. In 1960, when she came back to Hollywood to film *Flaming Star,* she said, "I took the role because it permitted me to play an intelligent, sensitive woman of character."

Of the handful of Great Stars from the Silent Screen who survive today, Dolores Del Rio is possibly the least known to contemporary audiences. A few of her silent pictures, *What Price Glory, The Loves of Carmen* and *The Red Dance,* can be seen occasionally in museum showings in New York, London, Paris and Moscow. Some of her talkies, *Wonder Bar, Journey into Fear* and, principally, *Flying Down to Rio* (in which *she* starred, supported by the then new team of Astaire and Rogers), are revived from time to time.

Today's film aficionados may know her best from her two John Ford movies, *The Fugitive* with Henry Fonda and *Cheyenne Autumn,* and from *Flaming Star* with Elvis Presley. In the latter, playing Presley's Indian mother, she was highly praised for "a performance of controlled intensity."

When her old friend, salty John Ford, lured her back to Hollywood in 1947, he said, "Dolores has developed into a great star. She is the best-loved actress in Mexico and we feel very fortunate to be able to get her. Every company in Mexico sits on her doorstep." She and Ford were mutual admirers from the 30's when he used to play tennis at her Santa Monica home.

The Fugitive was a splendid, highly praised movie that also did well at the box office. In the New York *Times,* Bosley Crowther wrote, ". . . a strange and haunting picture. . . . Mr. Ford has accomplished in it a true companion to his *The Informer.* The performances are all excellent. . . . Del Rio is a warm glow of devotion as an Indian Magdalene. Let us thank Mr. Ford for one of the best pictures of the year."

When, at age fifty-eight, Del Rio came back to Hollywood for Ford's *Cheyenne Autumn,* it marked a return to Warner Bros. where she had been under contract in the 30's. She recalled, "I did so many pictures in Hollywood, but I can remember the names of only a few. A lot of us started here in 1925—Joan Crawford, Constance Bennett, Myrna Loy and Gary Cooper. And I."

Dolores Del Rio in 1928, and 1944 through 1960. Her beauty continues to defy time and classification.

Her jewelry collection is fabulous. "Pearls are my passion. For daytime, I never wear any other gems. And at night, my jewels are rubies." Pictured here are some examples of her legendary collection of pearls, rubies and diamonds.

The small mole to the left of Del Rio's nose was, at first, covered over by makeup in films. Later, she made a sort of beauty mark out of this distinctive feature. It can be seen throughout this chapter.

At the door of her home in the elegant Mexico City suburb of Coyancán, a home she describes as "Mexican—but modern!" In the garden is a bronze bust of her by Costa Rican sculptor Francico Zoniga, and inside are many portraits of Del Rio painted through the years by leading artists including Adolfo Best, Roberto Montenegro and José Clemente Orozco. (Diego Rivera executed a sitting pose.) Del Rio poses here in 1940 alongside a portrait by Rosa Covarrubias, and looks at another work with artist John Carroll.

Del Rio and her husband, Lewis Riley, are enthusiastic collectors of pre-Columbian art and their home boasts a large and varied assemblage of statues and artifacts—delicate figures from the funeral island of Jaina and idols from Colima and Nayarit. Separating the multifold books on their library shelves are statues from Oaxaca and Vera Cruz.

HAIR STYLES

Del Rio in *The Queen and the Rebels* by Ugo Betti

Del Rio in stage makeup

ON STAGE

As early as 1930, Del Rio declared her aspiration to go on the stage. "I'd love to appear in fine, emotional dramas . . . and am eager to play in stories concerning my native people, the Mexican race. It is my dearest wish to make fans realize their real beauty, their wonder, their greatness as a people. The vast majority seem to regard Mexicans as a race of bandits, or laborers, dirty, unkempt and uneducated. My ambition is to show the best that's in my nation."

It wasn't until 1956 that she finally realized her ambitions when she debuted in *Anastasia* in a summer stock tour of various cities in New England. Buoyed up by the experience, she took special classes in the theater technique with Stella Adler in New York City and made her first appearance on the Mexican stage in 1958 in Oscar Wilde's *Lady Windermere's Fan*, which she had filmed in 1948 in Buenos Aires. Since

then, her stage plays have included *The Road to Rome, The Little Foxes, A Month in the Country, La Vidente,* Ugo Betti's *The Queen and the Rebels* and as Mrs. Patrick Campbell in *Dear Liar*. She was playing in Ibsen's *Ghosts* in 1962 in her native Mexico City when her beloved mother died, but she continued her performances, to the deep appreciation of the Mexican people, who understood and applauded her gallantry.

For her many stage activities in Mexico and other Latin countries, she is titled "First Lady of the Mexican Theater" and was so honored by Helen Hayes, who journeyed from New York to Mexico City to bestow the award. She was most recently seen as Margarita in a Mexico City production of *La Dama de las Camelias* in which she broke all house records, an achievement she duplicated with *Dear Liar*.

Del Rio with her three husbands:

Jaime del Rio in 1927 (married in 1921 and divorced in December 1928). He died later that same year.

Cedric Gibbons in 1935 (married in 1930 and divorced in 1941)

Lewis A. Riley, whom she married in 1959

ON MEXICO

Octavio Paz, the renowned Mexican poet and essayist, has written, "Stoicism is the highest Mexican virtue . . . from childhood, we are taught to accept defeat and disappointment with dignity." This manner of thinking was undoubtedly a contributing factor to the way Del Rio reacted to her many career disappointments. It enabled her, seemingly unruffled, to continue to pursue her goals and, when it became necessary, to return to her native land to do so.

Her father, to whom she was very close, died in 1940. The next year she divorced Cedric Gibbons. With both her career and emotional life in a spin, she sold her home in Hollywood in 1942 and returned to Mexico where she created in Mexican films a new movie personality—a subtle mixing of the more measured and restricted style imposed on her in Hollywood with the fire and passion inherent in the Latin blood. She became an outstanding star who was the essence of Latin America, the First Lady of Mexican Cinema.

In *Time,* the December 8, 1958, article on Mexico in "The Hemisphere" section, spoke of the new Mexico with its outstanding citizens, including "such cultured artists as Dolores Del Rio, who found big audiences and vast popularity among the new middle class."

In the past two decades, Del Rio has received many awards and honors. In 1966, she went to Spain to pick up her Quixote, the Spanish equivalent of the Oscar, for her performance in *La Dama del Alba.* Then, in 1976, she returned to Madrid for a film festival dedicated to her Hollywood and Spanish-speaking movies. In her native country, she has four times been awarded the Ariel, Mexico's Oscar, for *Flor Silvestre* in 1943, *Las Abandonadas* in 1944, *Dona Perfecta* in 1950, and *El Nino y la Niebla* (which won eight Ariels overall). She is shown here in *Flor Silvestre* with Pedro Armendariz and in *Las Abandonadas.*

Among her other Latin films were: *Lady Windermere's Fan* made in Argentina in 1948 and released in the United States as *Una Mala Mujer; Bugamblia,* 1944, and *Maria Candelaria* with Pedro Armendariz, 1943; and *El Pecado de una Madre* with Libertad Lamarque.

It is unfortunate that so few of Del Rio's Mexican and European films of the past few decades, which rectified Hollywood's waste of her talent, have had any national showings outside of those countries, and that other audiences have been deprived of seeing her mature as a serious and dedicated artist. It accounts, of course, for the fact that today she is more a legend than a recognized star among younger audiences.

Flor Silvestre

Las Abandonadas

Bugamblia

Una Mala Mujer

Maria Candelaria

Speaking of beauty, Del Rio has said, "God can give us beauty, and genes can give us our features. But whether that beauty remains or changes is determined by our thoughts and deeds. We have the face *we* created over the years. For beauty does not come with creams and lotions—it comes with moderation in eating, good digestion, and discipline in life.

"I'm very much a person of today, I don't regret anything in the past, any of my mistakes. It's very foolish to live with regrets and I don't think I've done anything bad in the sense of wrong.

"I am not much for yesterday except for the lessons it has taught. So I live for now. There is so little time left and I still want to do so many things. There is still much to accomplish, roles I want to play, countries I still want to see. With so much I must do in the time I have left, time has become very precious to me."

Del Rio proves that beauty, true beauty, is not related to age but rather is a reflection of spirit and attitude—which enhance the whole look.

El Pecado de una Madre

RECENT YEARS

In recent years Del Rio has been immersed in social and cultural work. She has a special project, a nursery for children called Estancia Infantil, of which she is president of the board.

"Our nursery is the first of its kind in the world and our doors never close. Not even the socialist countries have such nurseries for children of working women. We are trying new ways of education with wonderful results after putting an enormous emphasis on music, ballet and singing."

In 1970, Del Rio made a rare appearance on the popular TV series, "Marcus Welby, M.D." She is pictured here with Janet Blair, who played her daughter in this episode, opposite.

In July 1967 she was saluted by Pecime, the Society of Mexican Cinematograph Reporters, at a special ceremony in Mexico City. At the event, which was attended by civic and theatrical notables, she was presented with a Silver Sarafe Trophy and Gold Medal in honor of her "forty years of artistic activity."

On March 15, 1977, it was announced that Del Rio and five other long-time personalities of Mexico, Maria Felix, Marga Lopez, Fernando Soler, Gabriel Figueroa and Sara Garcia, would participate in *To Laugh Crying*, a film following the pattern of *That's Entertainment*. It will be a fond memory with scenes from their most popular films, and interviews with them about their careers and the many personalities with whom they have worked.

Two weeks later, on March 28, Del Rio announced that she was coming back to make her first American film in a dozen years. She is to play opposite Anthony Quinn in *Children of Sanchez*.

The deaths of Joan Crawford, Rosalind Russell, Vivien Leigh, Miriam Hopkins, Jeanette MacDonald and Constance Bennett have diminished considerably the once abundant list of living Superstars. As vivid reminders of the 20's, 30's and 40's, we still have Lillian Gish, Gloria Swanson, Greta Garbo, Marlene Dietrich, Norma Shearer, Loretta Young, Claudette Colbert and Barbara Stanwyck, none of whom is currently active on screen. Only four ladies of this tome are actually still performing in films or on the stage. They are, of course, Del Rio, Loy, Hepburn and Davis. And it is to be hoped that they all will continue to grace the art of performing and to persist in their careers for many years to come, for the likes of them appear seldom in any century.

We can be grateful that the luminescent beauty and personality of Dolores Del Rio that brightened the gossamer world of Hollywood still can be seen on the screens of the world and in such photographs as are displayed throughout this chapter.

RÉSUMÉ

MYRNA LOY

In this age of instant stardom and short-lived Superstars, when one can see film after film "starring" someone never before seen or heard of, and whom, too often, one hopes never to see or hear of again, it *is* a surprise to recall that during Hollywood's peak years it took most actors and actresses about five years to reach screen stardom—a stardom that lasted from five to seven years if the performer was lucky.

With this in mind, the longevity of Myrna Loy's career becomes even more surprising and remarkable. It took her nine years and over seventy films to become a star and then only after a dishearteningly long apprenticeship playing a succession of oriental half-castes, South Sea native girls or the vampish "other woman."

When she entered films, the Silent Screen was at its height, and its Big Women Stars were perpetually pure ingenues Mary Pickford and Lillian Gish; sophisticated women of the world Gloria Swanson, Pola Negri and Mae Murray; Norma Talmadge and Corinne Griffith, who specialized in the sort of womanly roles that Loy and Irene Dunne were to play in the 30's and 40's; and the screen flapper, popularized by Colleen Moore and Clara Bow. Loy was like none of them, and for a long time stardom seemed a moot possibility until talking pictures enabled her to properly display her true personality and ability. It was only then, after that incredibly protracted period, that she joined the eminent and lofty group of Star-figures.

Her contract career began in 1926 at Warner Bros., which, even then, was primarily a man's studio. John Barrymore and Rin-Tin-Tin were its principal stars and the fairly interchangeable women's roles were shared by Irene Rich, May McAvoy, Marie Prevost, Leila Hyams, Audrey Ferris, Helene and Dolores Costello and Loy. Warner Bros. seldom tried to build a woman star and were not particularly successful when they did: at the urging of her new husband, John Barrymore, Dolores Costello was given premature—and short-lived—stardom in the late 20's. This unsuccessful experiment was repeated a short time later when another Barrymore leading lady, Marian Marsh, was given her stardom too early. Only Bette Davis, of the studio's contract players in the 30's, became a star; Kay Francis and Ruth Chatterton, both established stars, were acquired from Paramount in the 30's as, of course, was Joan Crawford from M-G-M in the 40's. And only after winning her freedom from Warners in a court battle did Olivia de Havilland attain solo stardom.

In 1929, Warner Bros. combined with First National Pictures and this brought Loretta Young, Dorothy Mackaill, Alice White and others into the organization, further diminishing Loy's opportunities for better roles. She left Warners in 1930 and her career slowly began to improve as a few worthy parts came her way leading to a contract in 1932 with M-G-M. Stardom belatedly arrived in 1934, nine years after she entered films.

I was able to see a remarkable number of Loy's early pictures while researching this book: such silents as *Pretty Ladies, Ben Hur, Don Juan, When a Man Loves* and *Noah's Ark,* and embryonic talkies like *The Jazz Singer, The Desert Song, Show of Shows, The Black Watch* and *The Truth About Youth.* I observed her interesting switch into more human roles in *Transatlantic, Rebound, Arrowsmith, Emma* and *The Wet Parade.* And when I saw *Love Me Tonight, Penthouse, Thirteen Women* and *The Barbarian* and observed her unlimited variations of interpretation, it was clearly evident that stardom was forthcoming.

Watching her during her peak years at M-G-M in *Night Flight, Men in White, Manhattan Melodrama, The Thin Man* series, *Wings in the Dark, Wife vs. Secretary, The Great Ziegfeld, Libeled Lady* (so superior to its very good remake), *Test Pilot, The Rains Came, Love Crazy* and others gave me a deepening appreciation of Loy's subtlety, never ending versatility and always seemingly effortless underplaying. How very deserving she is of the critical praise heaped on her, something that cannot be said of some of her contemporaries when their old films are seen and re-evaluated today. That Loy has remained a star for over forty years is evidence of her talent, intelligence and adaptability.

Among Hollywood's most famous redheads, Myrna Loy always occupies a prominent place. And properly so, since not only is she among the most outstanding in that group but, more importantly, she is one of the few *authentics.* In each decade the movies had a reigning redhead: Clara Bow as the most celebrated of the 20's, Loy the most eminent of the 30's, Rita Hayworth was the most notable of the 40's and Lucille Ball the most renowned during the 50's and 60's. But what is most interesting about this group is that, with the exception of Loy, none were really redheads! All dyed for their art.

For many years, particularly during the days when films were shot in black and white, red hair presented a problem to the camera: it photographed dark or black, so such genuine redheads as Nancy Carroll and Ginger Rogers became blondes for camera purposes. In the 20's when Klieg lights were used, cameramen had found that henna gave highlights to dark hair, which was hard to photograph becomingly. Many actresses used a henna rinse and among those who tried it and found it an improvement was the then relatively unknown Clara Bow. From there, she went to a flashy, flaming red and then finally to the red-gold she kept for the remainder of her career. It was a different story, however, for such stars as Dietrich, Jeanette MacDonald and Greer Garson, all of whom had natural red-gold hair. On camera, their hair photographed too dark and drab, so they switched to blonde—the shade most becoming to them on screen.

Rita Hayworth, originally a Latin brunette, had her appearance considerably altered after she was signed by Columbia Pictures. A series of tests and apprenticeship films led to long and painful electrolysis treatments that broadened her forehead: then her hair was dyed red for the Technicolor films *Blood and Sand* and *Strawberry Blonde*. As a redhead, she was a sensation and a new glamour pin-up girl was born. Similarly, M-G-M turned the blonde Lucille Ball into a flaming redhead for *Ziegfeld Follies* and *Best Foot Forward*, and redheaded Jeanette MacDonald, who became a blonde for black and white films, was transformed back into a Technicolor redhead. There seems to be no current successor to Loy, Bow, Hayworth et al., and films certainly could use a glamorous, exciting redhead to brighten today's screens.

Seeing Myrna Loy in person these days, she appears much younger and more beautiful than some of her recent photographs would indicate. Black and white photography does not do her justice—color is really required! The famous red hair is as glorious as ever, the twinkling eyes and radiant smile just as overpowering. She doesn't turn on the charm but it is there, subtle and quiet, and the combination of all this is quite devastating.

We got together a number of times during the preparation of this book, and one day I read her a quote from a 20's interview in which she allegedly said, "I became known as an American girl gone native in an Easterly direction."

"Did I ever really say that?" she laughed with that dry-martini voice and crinkling those unique eyes. We were discussing her early career, "when I played wretched women with knives in their teeth!" stereotyped in roles of slinky, sloe-eyed sirens who personified sex in a lurid but limited range. As one looks at photographs of her during that phase of her career, it seems amazing that she was so successfully able to change her screen type in an almost overnight switch from those vamps and half-caste native girls to her enduring image of "perfect wife" and "ideal American woman."

Actually, the metamorphosis took nearly nine years, a long apprenticeship during which she worked constantly in a steady variety of roles learning every aspect of her craft. When finally she got her memorable role of Nora Charles in *The Thin Man,* she was well prepared for it and for the deserved success that followed.

Overnight, Loy seemed to be practically everyone's favorite actress. She became the epitome of a new type of sophistication—a distinct change from Garbo, Crawford or Shearer on her home lot at M-G-M, and an equal contrast to her contemporaries Davis, Hepburn and Lombard at other studios. Metro was not prepared for the unexpected success of *The Thin Man* (after all, it was just a mystery-comedy filmed on a low budget with no studio exploitation) nor for the sensational success she achieved because of it. The studio's adjustment to her increasing popularity and status seemed a bit leisurely, but, once it got under way, no other studio could surpass Metro's genius for the Star build-up. Wisely, they continued casting her in roles consistent with her newly discovered image. But now they were Star roles in important pictures in which she played opposite the biggest male names on the lot—Gable, Powell, Tracy, Robert Montgomery and Robert Taylor.

Within three years Loy was proclaimed "Queen of the Movies" in a poll conducted by Ed Sullivan for the public's nomination for that title. (Clark Gable was King.) Both won by large margins and Loy says, "I still have that crown they gave me somewhere." In 1937 and 1938 she was among the "Top Ten Best Box Office Stars," a list compiled by the Motion Picture Exhibitors. Along with Garbo, Shearer, Crawford, Harlow and MacDonald, she had reached the upper echelon of M-G-M's famed "More Stars Than There Are in Heaven."

Today she speaks warmly and affectionately of old friend William Powell, with whom she had "Hollywood's most successful celluloid marriage," and also of Joan Crawford, Jean Harlow, Ann Harding, Melvyn Douglas, Clark Gable and Tyrone Power. She is enthusiastic when she discusses directors Woody Van Dyke, Rouben Mamoulian, William Wyler and John Ford, and friends like Sam Goldwyn. "I will say one thing for the old days, we had individuality. I admire some of the people on the screen today but most of them look like everybody else. As to those 'monsters' I used to work with, well, I wish they were back. They really loved film and I miss them."

The past few decades, her time has been split between politics and her career. She is still active on stage, on TV and in films like *The End* with Burt Reynolds. She also is still lovely, still enchanting and still lively. Loy remains a skillful and adroit actress, a warm and admirable woman and a truly Fabulous Face.

Myrna Loy at the age of three months, and at ten with her cousin, Laura Bell.

She was born in Helena, Montana, on August 2, 1905, to David and Della Johnson Williams, and is of Scottish and Welsh descent. "Father died when I was quite young, leaving my mother with two small children [Myrna and a younger brother, David]. The Montana winters were rigorous, so she decided to move the family to California; we had gone there on several occasions during past winters and loved it.

"We settled in Culver City—then just a hamlet—and I worked in a neighborhood school of expression for children, after school, where I taught dancing and made my own costumes. I went to Westlake School for Girls, then to Venice High School, but I didn't like it, so after a year I got a job dancing in the chorus of Sid Grauman's Prologues at the Egyptian Theater."

While she was in Union High School in Venice, H. F. Weinbrener, a sculptor who was head of the art department, saw her dance and asked her to pose for a full-length statue that he named "Aspiration." It still stands in the schoolyard.

Photographer Henry Waxman had noticed the very pretty and totally different young Myrna Williams while she was dancing at the Egyptian Theater. He asked her to pose for some pictures which turned out so well that he displayed them in his gallery. They attracted some attention and led to her discovery by Rudolph Valentino and a change in her name.

"I liked my real name, Myrna Williams, so I didn't want to change it. But my friends kept telling me that there were already too many Williamses in the movies, Kathlyn Williams, Earle Williams, etc. Someone suggested "Myrna Lisa" but I thought that was ridiculous. Peter Rurick, a writer, really rechristened me. He had been in Henry Waxman's studio one day when I was there and, after looking at my pictures, also told me I should change my name. 'Williams' was okay for a little girl from Montana, but it didn't fit the girl in the pictures Henry had made of me. Not exotic enough, he protested. I thought that pretty funny because I knew that I, the real me, wasn't a bit exotic.

"He suggested the name 'Loy,' which he took from a book of Chinese poems and insisted that it suited my personality and horoscope and everything else. So I wrote Myrna Loy on the back of some photographs I submitted to Warner Bros. and, when I signed there shortly after, it became my name for good. 'Myrna Loy,' of course, turned out to be a wonder name for me and I love it."

About that time, Rudolph Valentino and his wife, Natacha Rambova, also noticed the Waxman pictures of Loy. Then the most important and romantic male star in Hollywood, Valentino's appearance in such hits as *The Four Horsemen, The Sheik, Blood and*

55

Sand and *Monsieur Beaucaire* had made him the idol of millions of women all over the world. Mrs. Valentino, who exerted a strong influence on her husband, was one of the most interesting women in Hollywood during the mid-20's. A distinct personality in her own right, she was daring, original and independent. Her knowledge of literature, music, painting and dance, plus her striking and unusual set and costume designs for her husband's films, caused many people to consider her a genius. Mrs. Valentino's familiarity with ballet undoubtedly was responsible in part for her interest in the young dancer, Myrna Loy.

"She was so beautiful, absolutely glorious, and so very kind to me. The first time we met, she was wearing a heavy, chocolate-brown velvet dress and turban she had designed. She always wore the most striking clothes, always those unusual turbans wound around her head; I never remember seeing her without one as long as I knew her. She brought her own clothes to the studio and lent them to me for a screen test they made of me for a picture called *Cobra* which Valentino planned to make. They both were just marvelous to me . . . but I didn't get the role—I was too skinny and far too inexperienced for such a part. I knew nothing about screen makeup and had never done any film acting, so the role went to Gertrude Olmstead. Later on, when Mrs. Valentino decided to do a film of her own called *What Price Beauty,* she gave me a role in it and also hired the then unknown Gilbert Adrian to assist her with the clothing designs.

"I was cast as 'The Intellectual Type' and Natacha dressed me in red velvet pajamas—long-sleeved, very tight and high at the throat. She arranged my hair in a cap effect with points on my forehead, slanted my eyes and, unquestionably, that bizarre role was the beginning of my career. It was not a popular or successful picture but it was a marvelous experience for me and, shortly after that, I signed a contract with Warner Bros."

What Price Beauty has a dream sequence in which the heroine wanders through a highly modernistic beauty parlor observing the models who are wearing clothes and coiffures to illustrate various types of beauty. Loy was dressed and coiffed as she described, wearing tailored red velvet pajamas and a blonde wig. She and Adrian, who designed some of the clothes, were to be reunited seven years later when she joined M-G-M in 1932.

Loy's real film career began in 1925, with bit parts in *Pretty Ladies* and *Ben Hur* at the newly formed M-G-M studios. At that time, Mae Murray and Lillian Gish were the studio's biggest women stars, with Norma Shearer, Eleanor Boardman, Aileen Pringle and Renée Adorée getting most of the leading-lady roles. That same year, two young unknowns were signed by M-G-M: Greta Garbo arrived from Sweden and Joan Crawford (then Lucille Le Sueur) from New York. Crawford and Loy worked together in *Pretty Ladies,* and when Loy returned to Metro in '32 as a contract player, Crawford, Garbo and Shearer were the studio's top female attractions. Within a relatively short time, Loy herself was to become a part of the studio's top echelon.

I asked Miss Loy whether this picture (top left, p. 58), taken at M-G-M in 1925, was from *Ben Hur* or *Pretty Ladies:*

"I'm not sure, I think Erté did that costume, so it might be *Pretty Ladies.* But I remember wearing that wig when I was being considered for the part of the Madonna in *Ben Hur.* Since I was also playing another small role in the chariot race sequence, they put that wig on me to give me an entirely different look from the Madonna.

"Henry Waxman precipitated the next turning point in my life: He took portraits of me as 'The Intellectual Type' in *What Price Beauty* and showed them to Warner Bros. The result was a part in *Satin in Sables* with Lowell Sherman (top right, p. 58). It was only a bit for me but a very showy one and, on the strength of it, I got my first contract with Warners in 1925."

During the silent picture era, Warner Bros. was uncertain as how best to use Loy. Her exotic screen appearance was such a distinct contrast to the prevailing mode of leading ladies that she was assigned "a lead in one film and then a bit in the next . . . sometimes practically an extra bit! I was lucky to get a closeup in those early days. I started as a vamp although I was given an occasional lead, usually in a B picture. Most of the time I was cast as an exotic because I had been a dancer and could slink. A contract player had to expect that sort of thing then; we had no union and they'd work us for many long hours . . . day and night . . . sometimes in two or three pictures at the same time."

This is the very first picture of Myrna Loy ever printed in a national magazine, and it appeared in the August 1925 *Motion Picture.* It's interesting now to read the copy written about the then unknown young dancer who, ten years later, was to become one of the screen's biggest attractions.

Henry Waxman

Myrna Loy

There's a great buzzing and roaring in our ears: It's the thousands upon thousands of readers asking "Who . . . is . . . she? Who Is She? Whoisshe?" Well, she's what Mrs. Rudolph Valentino says is going to be the 1926 flapper model. You'll see her first in "What Price Beauty," Natacha Rambova Valentino's much-talked-about picture. Perhaps the word that best describes her type is "piquant" —or maybe "elfin." She's boyish—but bashfully boyish. She's lithe, and vivacious—but not muscular or "full of pep." She's the essence of grace; she is aloof; elusive; mysterious; sensitive. You dont know whether she's innocent or sophisticated; whether she's a low-brow or a high-brow; whether she's pretty or plain. But you do know that she is very, very young; and very, very fascinating. All you obvious, breezy, tom-boyish 1925 flapper models had better practise changing your type, or on New Year's day you'll find yourselves frightfully out of date

The vogue for oriental vampires was so popular that Loy appeared as Indian, Chinese, Japanese, Filipino, Polynesian and even mulatto sirens before she finally escaped that mold.

Seen here: Roles in *The Crimson City*, '28 (top left), *Across the Pacific*, '26 (top right) and *The Desert Song*, '29.

Loy: "I see the same thing still happening today. Young people get miscast—stuck with the wrong images and playing the wrong roles. People are so blind."

Some of Loy's directors were impressed by her obvious intelligence and hard work; she learned quickly and showed an aptitude for bigger and more versatile roles. Among those who tried to encourage and guide the young Loy was Lewis Milestone, who directed her in *Cave Man* and who was to direct *All Quiet on the Western Front* a few years hence. "I worked again with him years later (1949) in *The Red Pony* with Bob Mitchum. Alan Crosland liked me, said he thought I had a future and kept pushing me for bigger roles. And Michael Curtiz [*Noah's Ark*] became interested in me and told me he thought I should play Madame Bovary.

"But [Darryl F.] Zanuck, who was in charge of studio production then, couldn't see me as anything but a vamp. So when my contract came up for renewal, he decided I'd never go any further and let me go. In a TV interview recently, when he was asked to comment about mistakes in judgment during his career, he mentioned firing me at Warners. It's funny now because nine years later, when he was head of 20th Century-Fox, he borrowed me from M-G-M for the lead in *The Rains Came* with Ty Power. But there again, I was really a femme fatale! I don't think he could ever see me in any other type of role."

"But the camera seems to emphasize my peculiarities so that I'm not really convincing as an American. But what of that? There is a wealth of other material, and America is just a small place in the field of drama. Literature isn't bounded on the north by the ingenue —or on the south by the flapper."

(By 1935, Myrna Loy was the world's idea of the perfect American wife!)

Loy and Audrey Ferris as chorus girls in the 1927 film *The Jazz Singer* in which Al Jolson introduced song and dialogue to the screen (opposite, top left).

In 1927, Roy Del Ruth, who directed her in four films, *Across the Pacific, Ham and Eggs at the Front, If I Were Single* and *The Desert Song,* said of Loy: "In appearance, she is startling; tall, graceful, with an ease of movement acquired through years of dancing . . . (she is) titian-haired, with almond-shaped eyes as green as the sea and just as baffling—eyes whose curling lashes shadow wisdom and mystery."

In an interview with Margaret Reid in the June 1927 issue of *Picture Play* magazine, Loy was quoted as saying: "I'm quite aware that I don't look American on the screen. Off screen with all my freckles, I look more what I really am—Myrna Williams, born in Montana.

60

A rare glimpse of the real and unaffected Loy is given in this portrait from *Under a Texas Moon*, 1930 (left).

That same year she appeared in *Cameo Kirby*, playing the mistress of villain Douglas Gilmore (above).

Myrna Loy in two portraits from *Bride of the Regiment,* 1930, in which her costumes were designed by Earl Luick. When I showed her these photographs she exclaimed, "Those clothes were so fantastic—absolutely beautiful! That dress was salmon-colored, I think." Luick recalls watching Loy on the set, looking soignée and most sophisticated. "I'd say, 'Let's have lunch. I'll meet you in the commissary.' She'd agree, go change into her own clothes and in would come this sweet, unassuming girl who could have been a college student. She was almost naïve in her attitude. It was hard to believe she was the same person I'd watched earlier."

Vivienne Segal and Walter Pidgeon had the singing lead in this operetta, which was based on *The Lady in Ermine* and filmed in color. Loy played the supporting role of Sophie, the "other woman"!

When she was cast time and again as a wicked woman, a vamp or some half-caste sorceress, Loy began to study the character, the psychology and even the religion of the role she was to play. "Since I never quite believed in them, I had to attribute some sort of phobia to the characters so they would seem more real. I had to understand how and why anyone could be like that in order to make them convincing on the screen. Now, villains are much more interesting—they're no longer black and white characters."

Loy became so proficient in these roles that she was very nearly limited to playing them forever. To counteract her restricted opportunities, she earnestly set about seeking other types of women to play.

Loy won the "Honor Page" in the August 1929 issue of *Screenland* magazine for her acting in *The Black Watch* and *The Squall,* which were selected as "the best performances of the month." Editor Delight Evans wrote: (Myrna Loy is) "Caviar, not corned beef and cabbage. Like [Ronald] Colman Myrna Loy is subtle. She is quiet but clever . . . optical and audible charm incarnate. The lovely Loy lady comes into her own in *The Squall.* She is sensational as well in *The Black Watch.*" Such recognition was a big help in advancing her career.

Had pictures remained silent, Loy might have stayed a supporting player or leading lady. But with the advent of talking pictures the Loy voice, which came to be recognized as a valuable adjunct of her charm and personality, was an important asset in changing her image from exotic vamp to real woman. It had color, humor and character. Combined with the twinkle in her eyes, ready laugh and satin growl, it helped her true personality to emerge. Here, obviously, was no foreign menace but a well-bred young American lady!

1929

1934

Here is Loy as the evil Yasmini in *The Black Watch* with Roy D'Arcy (left, top and bottom).

Her ability to wear fantastic clothes and towering headdresses with ease and poise made Loy a valuable asset to such films as *A Connecticut Yankee in King Arthur's Court* and *Mask of Fu Manchu.*

After being dropped by Warner Bros. in 1931, Loy signed with Fox studios, who gave her somewhat better roles. If she still was assigned an occasional role as vamp or exotic, she was able to play it with more humor and style. She even got a sympathetic straight role as the wife in *Transatlantic* to contrast with the genteel home wrecker in *Rebound,* the mistress in *Skyline* or the husband's girl friend in *Consolation Marriage.* As her parts and films improved in quality, her popularity grew and a long-overdue change in her career began.

Arthur Hornblow, Jr. (later to be her first husband), became interested in her as did director Rouben Mamoulian. Hornblow cast her in the prestigious *Arrowsmith* with Ronald Colman and Helen Hayes. Mamoulian gave her the role of a man-hungry countess in *Love Me Tonight* with Maurice Chevalier and Jeanette MacDonald. Her sly comedy performance

was a revelation to everyone. "I'd had a few dates with Mamoulian for theater and opera, and we became friends. He told me of a new film he was preparing and said, 'There's a part in it I think you could play. The studio said it was unnecessary and wants me to cut it out of the picture. But I need it as a foil for the Jeanette MacDonald role. Will you trust me and play it?'"

"Well, I did trust him so I said okay and went to work for him. Each day my lines, which were on special blue pages not in the regular script, would be delivered to me on the set and we'd shoot these scenes. After a week he showed the producers what he'd done and they said, 'Yes, go ahead with her.' So that is how I happened to play my first real comedy role, and it opened up a new career for me."

By this time, at the interested urging of Irving Thalberg, M-G-M had placed Loy under contract. Thalberg was extremely instrumental in building the careers of a number of stars, particularly Garbo and Norma Shearer, his wife. "He was very interested in the development of my career and asked me to come

With Ron Colman, far left; Max Baer and Walter Huston, right; and Jeanette MacDonald and Maurice Chevalier, bottom

see him. I was quite shy then but he did a great thing for me which helped me tremendously: he told me that he felt there was 'something between me and the audience' (he made a gesture like a veil or curtain), and that he wanted me to break through that. 'You must have confidence,' he explained. And he was right. Soon after that, something did happen to me and I learned to battle for the roles I wanted to play."

An important breakthrough occurred when Loy got the role of the warm and sympathetic prize-fighter's wife in *The Prizefighter and the Lady* opposite Max Baer. Her adroit performance aroused additional interest in her from both the public and her studio, who assigned her more good roles that year: *When Ladies Meet, Night Flight* and *Men in White*. All added laurels to her fast-rising career. Then in 1934 she made two films that were to change the entire course of her professional life. First came *Manhattan Melodrama* with William Powell and Clark Gable, followed immediately by *The Thin Man*. In both, she was a sexually desirable woman who deferred to her man with grace, charm and calm acceptance instead, as in her former parts, of selfishly using him. Suddenly—she was a Star—and an important one.

During the next ten years she and Powell were teamed in thirteen films and their pairing was described as "Hollywood's most successful celluloid marriage." Certainly, it lasted longer than many of the real ones! Equally popular and successful were her six films with Clark Gable.

This change in image was one about which both the public and the critics were enthusiastic; Loy joined that select group, the box office "Top Ten," in 1937 and '38.

With Leslie Howard in *The Animal Kingdom*

One of Myrna Loy's most favorite directors (and best friends) was W. S. (Woody) Van Dyke, with whom she made eight films. She worked for him first in *The Prizefighter and the Lady,* closely followed by *Penthouse.* "I then played a part for him in *Manhattan Melodrama,* which was the first time I ever worked with Bill [Powell]. I was sort of a moll in it and, by then, Woody had become a champion of mine. He'd go into the studio commissary and proclaim, 'She's going to be a star. In a year, she'll be a Big Star.' When he asked for me in *The Thin Man,* they said he was crazy. But he answered, 'No, she'll be okay—I've thrown her in the pool.' (When you went over to his house, that was his test for you.) So he felt I could do it."

She *did* do it and, as everybody knows, the picture catapulted her into the stardom predicted for her by Van Dyke.

With Robert Young (television's Marcus Welby) in *New Morals for Old*

In 1926 she had a small role in *Don Juan,* which starred John Barrymore, who was then at the height of his career and fame. I asked, "What was he like then?" and she laughed, "He used to scare me to death. I was terribly shy and he'd call me up in the middle of the night and tease me. Of course, at that time he was quite a ladies' man and he hadn't yet married Dolores [Costello]. He frightened me but he *was* attractive!"

Barrymore and Loy worked together subsequently in 1933 when she was his leading lady in *Topaze* (above). I wondered, "How did you find him by that time?"

"Oh, he was charming," she replied. "That was eight years later; he'd married and settled down a great deal. We had great fun with *Topaze* and you might be amused at something that occurred before we began shooting: I hadn't seen Barrymore for quite a while; we'd had a little misunderstanding some

years earlier and I wondered if he'd remember it or whether it would have any effect on the new film. The night before we began shooting, I had to go over to RKO to discuss some things with our director, Harry D'Arrast.

"Just as I came in the studio, Barrymore was leaving and he looked straight at me as he went by but didn't say hello. When I got to the set, D'Arrast welcomed me and told me how much he and John were looking forward to working with me. I said, 'I don't know, he just passed me without speaking!' Harry reassured me, 'Oh no, he really wants you for the picture.'

"Well, the next morning as I was getting made up, there was a knock on my dressing-room door. It was Barrymore. He said, 'Myrna, I want to apologize for last evening. I saw you, but there were three of you and I didn't know which one to bow to.' "

Here she is seen with Louis B. Mayer, M-G-M's studio head, after signing her new contract. Although the studio used Roz Russell principally as a "threat" to Loy during the period of her contract dispute, that ploy never affected their friendship. After Loy

achieved her aim, Russell went on to become a personality and star in her own right, and they played together in the 1938 film *Man-Proof* with Walter Pidgeon (left) and Franchot Tone (right).

Loy's rise to stardom was accomplished with the help of critics and magazine editors who perceived her potential long before her producers did. Delight Evans, the bright and oft-quoted editor of *Screenland* magazine, was a long-time champion of hers. She plugged her for stardom as early as 1929 on her editorial pages (as discussed earlier) and continued to do so in her monthly film reviews.

On *Topaze,* May 1933: "Speaking of Myrna Loy and do let's, she manages somehow to score with the minimum number of closeups ever allotted a heroine. She is very smooth and sirenic, and I find myself wondering if her quiet but telling performance isn't a greater acting feat than [John] Barrymore's."

When Ladies Meet, September 1933: "You've never watched more polished and proficient acting than that offered by Ann Harding, Myrna Loy, Frank Morgan and Robert Montgomery . . . a knockout movie."

Men in White, June 1934: "The most perfect group acting of the month! The performances of Gable, Loy, Jean Hersholt and Elizabeth Allan remind you of the superb teamwork of a great acting company such as the Theatre Guild in its splendid co-ordination."

Manhattan Melodrama, July 1934: "More and more the Loy lady amazes me! Surely she is great star material."

The Thin Man, August 1934: "William Powell's debonair Nick is, perhaps, as finished and glittering a

performance as he or any other actor has contributed to the screen. Matching him stride for stride in his swiftly paced display of acting pyrotechnics is Myrna Loy as the fascinating, unconventional Nora."

And from *Film Daily:* "Miss Loy represents a very genuine and persuasive heroine—a very beautiful characterization."

Myrna Loy and William Powell (formerly the Silent Screen's oriental menace and its most suave villain) became talking pictures' foremost symbol of married love, advancing a fresh portrayal of marriage. Until then, for the most part, if a couple had any love life after marriage, the movies usually delicately declined to inquire what it was. Then came *The Thin Man.* As famed critic Gilbert Seldes observed, "The viewer wondered what on earth Nick, the detective, hoped to gain by making love to his own wife: and what was his wife after, wasting her time being in love with her own husband? Yet the picture *was* pleasing . . . and it said the one thing about love which the movies had hesitated to say for twenty years."

After the first *Thin Man,* there were five sequels: *After the Thin Man, Another Thin Man, Shadow of the Thin Man, The Thin Man Goes Home* and *Song of the Thin Man.* Loy and the urbane Powell also teamed successfully for six other films: *Manhattan Melodrama, Evelyn Prentice, The Great Ziegfeld, Double Wedding, I Love You Again* and *Love Crazy* —a total of thirteen films that made them the most

winning team in pictures. And the longest-running! Loy recalls that, in addition, "I did an unbilled bit as a gag in the last scene of [Powell's] *The Senator Was Indiscreet.*"

Loy and Powell were a debonair and amiable duo whose personal affection and admiration for each other has survived throughout the years. She says, "After I gave up oriental sirens, I played parts rather close to myself. From the very first scene Bill and I did together in *Manhattan Melodrama*, we felt that particular magic there was between us . . . a feeling of rhythm, complete understanding and an instinct of how each of us could bring out the best in the other." And, in an interview in the March 1936 *Screenland*, Powell said, "Any actor who has a chance to play opposite Myrna Loy is a lucky guy. *The Thin Man* would never have been the success it was without her. She has the give and take of acting that brings out the best. When we do a scene together, we forget about technique, camera angles and microphones. We aren't acting—we are just two people in perfect harmony. . . . Many times I've played with an actress who seemed to be separated from me by a plate-glass window; there was no contact at all. But Myrna, unlike some actresses who think only of themselves, has the happy faculty of being able to listen while the other fellow says his lines. She has learned that art—and is the 'best listener' I know."

Critic Bosley Crowther wrote in the New York *Times* of Loy and Powell, "They can make an hour and a half spin like a roulette wheel."

Loy and Cary Grant were teamed for *Wings in the Dark* in 1934, a picture about flying for which Amelia Earhart was the technical adviser. Loy had the part of stunt pilot on the circus circuit and Grant had that of an ambitious flier who, until he was blinded, hoped to shatter the world speed record. *Daily Variety*'s review said: "Myrna Loy, by many considered the most gracious lady of the screen, here fulfills every demand of her admirers and will continue, by virtue of her extraordinary performance, to add to her queue of fans. Her love scenes are superb . . . she is enchanting!"

Loy, pictured here as Billie
Burke in *The Great Ziegfeld*, is
dressed by Adrian and wearing
a light red wig.

The look, style and attitude of the Warner Bros. Loy, vamp and "other woman" in 1928, was perceptively changed by 1936 to the M-G-M image of Loy, everybody's "favorite wife" on the screen. The transformation of this suave actress from exotic to American woman was successfully copied by producer Samuel Goldwyn when he changed Merle Oberon from a foreign, sophisticated beauty into a lovely English-American type.

Before her stardom, Myrna Loy (along with Greta Garbo) was considered Hollywood's prime "mystery woman." She had been a shy, reticent person with few intimates who was unhappy in the spotlight. Also, her busy working schedule permitted little time for social life, so the "mystery woman" image was neither deliberate nor something contrived for publicity purposes. She lived quietly in a modest home with her mother and brother David, and as she battled her way to stardom (which took considerable drive, planning and determination: she *had to* break out of her vamp mold!). Her unobtrusive, even tranquil personal life gave little opportunity for the typical front-page existence led by some of her contemporaries. That would have been distasteful to her, anyway.

Loy was one of the busiest performers in films; no work was too difficult and no effort too much, if it would enhance the value of her performance. She had begun as a "bit player" in 1925 and by 1934 had made an astounding sixty-seven films, more than many stars make in their lifetimes. In order to capitalize on her tremendous popularity, M-G-M rushed her from one film to the next while they continued paying her the relatively low salary of an old contract. This problem was one many stars contended with then; Gable, Bette Davis, James Cagney and even Garbo had to fight it, each in his own style.

Loy, at that phase of her career, realized that she must slow down and make fewer and better films. Totally without temperament, she was the darling and delight of her directors and co-workers. But she also knew that her salary must be adjusted while she was at the top, for it never would be once her box office value slackened. So she asked for a salary adjustment commensurate with her status and for a long-overdue, deserved rest.

At that very time Rosalind Russell from the New York stage and Luise Rainer from Vienna arrived at M-G-M. Both profited by getting roles Loy turned down: Russell in *Rendezvous* and Rainer in *Escapade*. When, after several broken promises, the adjustments Loy sought were not forthcoming, she quietly packed her bags, boarded a plane and took the first vacation of her life in New York and Europe. Her good friends Ben Hecht and Charles MacArthur then took ads in the trade papers announcing that they were signing her to an exclusive contract, so M-G-M capitulated. Finally offered the contract she wanted, she returned to the studio and was met with open arms.

The Star build-up gets under way. Loy is photographed with M-G-M's veteran photographer Clarence Sinclair Bull, who took many of the Loy portraits in this book and who also was Garbo's favorite photographer. For magazines and newspapers, she is "seen in her garden," "at the beach home," and "dining out on a rare evening," with writer-producer Gene Markey, Hedy Lamarr and husband Arthur Hornblow. (Previously married to Joan Bennett and Hedy Lamarr, Markey was later to be Loy's third husband.)

PROFILES

Loy's profile and her unique turned-up nose were always a delight to photographers and cameramen. During the 30's and 40's, plastic surgeons said that the nose most often asked for by their women patients was the tilted one of Myrna Loy. Presumably, they hoped by acquiring the Loy nose to acquire also the Loy charm.

When I showed her these photographs, she laughed and said, "You know, in those days, everything had to be perfection in pictures: every hair in place, every eyelash on straight, no wrinkles in your clothes. David Selznick thought my ears stuck out too far and used to tease me about them. If I wore my hair up or swept back from my face, he'd have the makeup man glue them close to my head while a scene was being shot. As the lights got hotter, my ears would come unglued and pop loose and the director would say, 'Cut! Where's the makeup guy?' Then we'd have to start over again. It was so frustrating and tiring—I hated it.

"So one time when I was in New York, I went to a small private hospital to see a plastic surgeon. I forget if I went as 'Mrs. Hornblow' or 'Miss Williams,' but I didn't give my screen name. When I showed the doctor my ears and explained the problem, he said, 'Well, let's take some pictures and see what can be done.' So I pulled my hair up and he took photograph after photograph from every angle, even jumping up on a table and shooting down at me. I thought he was being awfully thorough!

"When he finally finished, he surprised me by saying, 'Thank you, Miss Loy. Now I have your nose from every angle! I get so many requests for a "Myrna Loy nose" that these pictures will be invaluable to me.' I burst into laughter and he went on, 'So I really shouldn't charge you anything should you decide you want to have your ears fixed.' I thanked him and said I'd think it over. But the next day was Pearl Harbor and I had to return immediately to the coast. So I didn't go back and never got my ears fixed!"

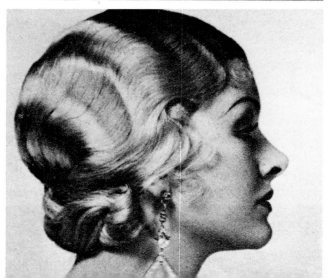

In 1936, Loy posed with artist James Montgomery Flagg, who drew the charcoal sketch of her for the cover of *Photoplay*.

While in London in 1949 to film *If This Be Sin*, she posed for a portrait by Cathleen Mann at the artist's Mayfair flat.

Clark Gable and Myrna Loy made six films together. After three very successful pictures, *Men in White, Manhattan Melodrama* (also with William Powell) and *Wife vs. Secretary,* the studio cast them in a costume drama about the life of Ireland's uncrowned king, *Parnell.* The result was a film few seem to have liked.

The next year M-G-M quickly reteamed them, plus Spencer Tracy, in *Test Pilot,* which turned out to be one of 1938's most popular films. *Cue* wrote, "Clark Gable, Spencer Tracy and Myrna Loy turn in probably the best performances of their careers, and help enormously to make this picture a leading contender for the Best Ten List of 1938," while *Box Office* said, "This one looks as if it's heading for wow grosses. In star value, it has Clark Gable, Myrna Loy and

Spencer Tracy and their performances rank well with anything they have so far done."

"I adored working on that one with Clark and Spence!" said Loy. "We all had nicknames: Clark called me 'Queenie,' we called him 'The King' and Spence was 'The Iron Duke.' I've forgotten why, but we dubbed [director] Vic Fleming 'The Monk.'"

Test Pilot was followed immediately by another Loy-Gable hit, *Too Hot to Handle,* also '38.

Of Clark Gable, Loy told me, "There was another side to him, a gentle one that was never publicized: he loved poetry. But that sort of thing didn't fit in with the image the studio was building for him, so few people were aware of it. But he trusted me and used to read me some of his favorite poems when we were together."

Loy with her mother, Mrs. Della Williams, at the première of *Wilson* in 1944. "Mother fostered my inclinations; she encouraged me to dance and played the piano for me when I had to audition. But she was never a stage mother—nor a busybody. She had a fit if she had to come to the studio—she hated all that fuss and never came unless specifically asked." Mrs. Williams apparently was very different from the average movie mother who stuck close to her daughter whenever possible to bask in her reflected glory.

As with Lombard, Del Rio and Davis, Myrna Loy was always very close to her mother and recalls:

"My mother was very interested in the arts. She had studied piano, seen all the theater she could while we were living in Montana and, after we moved to Los Angeles, we went to everything . . . symphony, opera, theater and ballet. We had tickets for all the great artists, the Philharmonic, the Hollywood Bowl. She was very influential in my life!

"I studied dancing while in high school and after graduation got a job in the chorus of Grauman's Egyptian Theater. I saw Pavlova dance *The Dying Swan*, the most magnificent performance I'd ever seen. No one else danced like that! And I saw Duse when she made her farewell appearance in 1924. I was anxious to become an actress, not just a dancer; so, after my last performance at the theater, a girl friend and I rushed all the way from Hollywood to downtown Los Angeles on the streetcar to see Duse. We came in late and our seats were in the balcony, way up high in the rafters. She was fantastic! I

remember that she wore no makeup, or so it seemed, and that she had gray-white hair. Although she was quite old at the time and died shortly afterwards, she played the role of a young woman, speaking entirely in Italian, which I didn't understand. But it didn't matter . . . she was overwhelming."

Always, Loy handled her career with calm assurance and a quiet determination to let none keep her in the secondary ranks. With an analytical, logical mind, she built for herself a steadfast career that met the requirements of her image and status. But there came the time when Loy realized that she was in danger of being typecast a second time and she definitely did not want that to happen.

Her transformation from vamp and oriental roles to "perfect wife" had been a difficult one, so she didn't intend to get caught again in a casting rut. Louis B. Mayer allegedly told her, "Whatever you play, you must always be a lady," and that sort of thinking by her studio eventually began to cause a problem in securing roles not always cut from the same cloth. Unsuccessfully, she tried for parts on loanout ("I wanted so badly to play *Love Story* with [Charles] Boyer but Irene Dunne got it"). But she did get a change of pace when 20th Century-Fox borrowed her to play the bored, unfaithful wife in *The Rains Came*. "There was a story that Louie Bromfield based his Lady Edwina in the book on Lady Mountbatten; they had been in India, you know. But I wasn't aware of the story when I played the role so it really didn't influence my conception of the part."

Those narrowed eyes that gazed rather disdainfully at the world in 1931 when Loy was still a screen vamp had long since regained a more normal, calm look by the time these portraits were made.

NA LOY- Metro Goldwyn-Mayer

After World War II, Loy returned to Hollywood in 1946 to resume her film career. Her first picture, *So Goes My Love* with Don Ameche, was quickly followed by one of the outstanding films of her career, *The Best Years of Our Lives.* A mature look at the return of servicemen to civilian life, their problems and readjustments, it was the first important postwar film and a smash hit. As the wife of Fredric March and mother of Teresa Wright and Michael Hall, Loy's beautiful performance was highly praised, and both she and author Robert E. Sherwood were awarded Grand Prizes at the World Festival of Films on June 3, 1947: she for the Best Feminine Performance of the Year, and he for the Best Screenplay.

She was "box office" again, and teamed with Cary Grant for two funny and successful pictures, *The Bachelor and the Bobby Soxer* (in which Shirley Temple played her sister) and *Mr. Blandings Builds His Dream House.* In '49 she made *The Red Pony* and the British *If This Be Sin,* and in '50, *Cheaper by the Dozen.* Her career continued with *Belles on Their Toes,* '52; *The Ambassador's Daughter,* '56; *Lonelyhearts,* '58; *From the Terrace* and *Midnight Lace,* '60; *The April Fools,* '69; the star-filled *Airport 75* and *The End,* which is her last film to date.

The Bachelor and the Bobby Soxer

Belles on Their Toes

Loy's old pictures are shown constantly on TV and at film revivals. Unlike those of some of her contemporaries, her performances do not become dated; the understated incisiveness and spontaneous gaiety of her acting make it seem as fresh today as when originally shown.

From the Terrace with Leon Ames, Rachel Stephens and Paul Newman

The Ambassador's Daughter

The April Fools

Loy and Powell in *After the Thin Man,* the second in a series of six *Thin Man* films

HUSBANDS

Myrna Loy was married four times; she is shown here with her first, second and third husbands: Arthur Hornblow, Jr. (top left), one of Hollywood's most prominent producers (*Ruggles of Red Gap, Gaslight, The Hucksters,* Carole Lombard's *Swing High, Swing Low, Midnight, Easy Living, Witness for the Prosecution,* etc.). They were married June 27, 1936, and divorced June 1, 1942.

Loy then married John Hertz, Jr. (top right), of Rent-A-Car fame, on June 8, 1942, but that marriage was short-lived.

In January 1946 she married an old friend, (then Commander) Gene Markey (bottom), at Terminal Island in San Pedro. Film director (then Captain) John Ford gave the bride away and Admiral William Halsey was best man. Markey was another prominent film producer and writer (who previously had been married to Joan Bennett, then Hedy Lamarr). They divorced in 1950.

On June 2, 1951 (a June bride for the third time!), Howland Sargeant, an assistant to Dean Acheson in the State Department, became her fourth husband. This marriage, her last, was terminated in May 1960, by divorce.

Loy's busy film career continued until 1941, when it was interrupted by World War II and her marriage to John Hertz, Jr. The couple moved to New York where she began working full time for the Red Cross, organizing entertainment for wounded soldiers and touring hospitals. In 1944 she returned to Hollywood to make her last contract picture for M-G-M, *The Thin Man Goes Home.* The studio planned it to be the final film of that series. She says, "Finding *The Thin Man* was an accident—a lucky one for me. But ten years of that kind of luck is enough." Despite her feelings, which were shared by Powell, the studio persuaded them to return in 1947 for one more appearance as Nick and Nora Charles in *Song of the Thin Man,* which was the swan song.

FASHION

Myrna Loy in her peak years was never a clotheshorse like Crawford, Lombard or Dietrich. So it *is* a revelation to see Loy, whose ladylike clothes came to be taken for granted, in some of the fantastic costumes and bizarre getups she wore with such style and authority during the early years of her career. After her transformation from exotic vamp to perfect wife, she wore tasteful clothes suited to the roles she was playing. By the time she became a major star, her screen clothes had become very un-Hollywood in their restraint, due in large part to the fact that Dolly Tree and not Adrian was designing most of them.

She speaks warmly and affectionately of Adrian, whom she first met when he helped dress her for Natacha Rambova's *What Price Beauty* in 1925. They were not reunited until she came to M-G-M in 1931. He designed her clothes for ten films made there: *Emma, The Wet Parade, Mask of Fu Manchu, The Barbarian, When Ladies Meet, Penthouse, Men in White, The Great Ziegfeld, Parnell* and *Double Wedding*. She says, "Adrian did marvelous things. But, at a preview of some film, I've forgotten which, Arthur [Hornblow, then her husband] said, 'I wish to God he'd stop putting those Big Buttons on you! They're too much for your face!' However, Adrian was busy with so many films and it really wasn't my choice who designed the clothes. But he was wonderful."

Dolly Tree was the designer for twelve of Loy's pictures during her M-G-M tenure. Her films with Loy were: *The Prizefighter and the Lady, Evelyn Prentice, Manhattan Melodrama, Stamboul Quest, The Thin Man, After the Thin Man, Libeled Lady, Wife vs. Secretary, Man-Proof, Test Pilot, Too Hot to Handle,* and *I Love You Again*. David Chierichetti, in his admirable, informative book, *Hollywood Costume Design*, wrote, "Loy's acting was powerful in its underplaying. If she wore clothes with too many clever details, they distracted from the subtlety of her performance. . . . The quiet sophistication of her films was more suited to Dolly Tree."

But during her overall career Loy's clothes *did* run the gamut, from bizarre and glamorous to dignified and subtly understated. Away from Metro, she was gowned by Earl Luick at Warner Bros., *The Desert Song* and *Bride of the Regiment*, Edith Head at Paramount, *Love Me Tonight* and *Wings in the Dark*, Howard Greer at RKO, *The Animal Kingdom* and Irene Sharaff at Goldwyn for *The Best Years of Our Lives* and *Midnight Lace*, and Christian Dior for *The Ambassador's Daughter*.

LEADING MEN

The monumental list of Myrna Loy's male co-stars includes: John Barrymore, Clark Gable, Spencer Tracy, William Powell, Walter Pidgeon, Victor McLaglen, Warner Baxter, Ronald Colman, Charles Farrell, Will Rogers, Edmund Lowe, Pat O'Brien, Neil Hamilton, Ralph Bellamy, Robert Young, Maurice Chevalier, Ricardo Cortez, Boris Karloff, Leslie Howard, Max Baer, Ramon Novarro, Walter Huston, Robert Montgomery, George Brent, Cary Grant, Franchot Tone, Robert Taylor, Tyrone Power, Melvyn Douglas, Don Ameche, Robert Mitchum, Clifton Webb, Adolphe Menjou, Montgomery Clift, Paul Newman, Rex Harrison, Charles Boyer and Jack Lemmon.

With Ramon Novarro

With Tyrone Power

With Warner Baxter

With Leslie Howard

With Neil Hamilton

With Robert Taylor

With George Brent

With Clark Gable

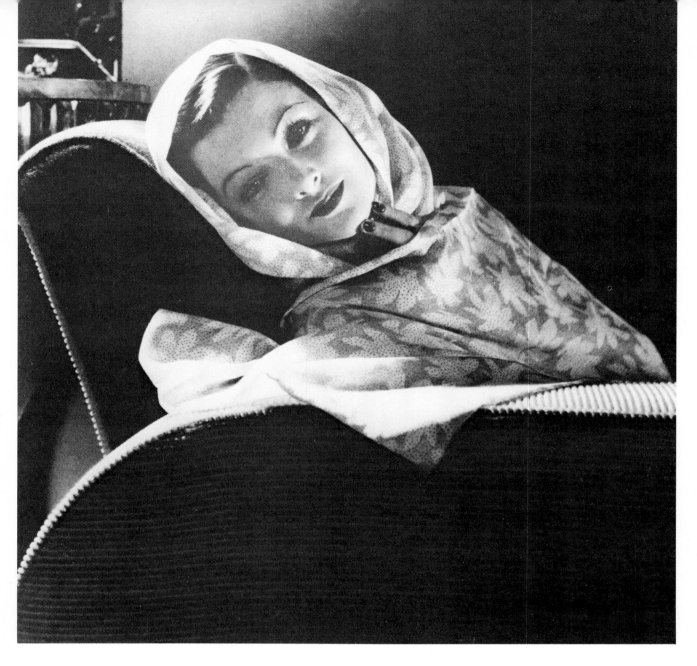

Melvyn Douglas and Loy played together in *Third Finger, Left Hand* (1940) and in *Mr. Blandings Builds His Dream House* (1948), and remained friends through the years. When they were reunited in 1971 for a television production of *Death Takes a Holiday,* Douglas told the press, "She's the only one from that period I'd really still enjoy seeing as a friend."

Loy: "I had lunch with Noel Coward one day and we were regretting that I never had the opportunity to play in any of his works: I would love to have done *Private Lives!* When he brought me home, we were standing in the lobby and he said the loveliest thing to me, 'Myrna, you never made a false move!' I was so touched, I ran upstairs and wrote it down. Imagine, Noel Coward saying that to me."

Apropos of Coward's compliment, it's fitting to recall that Loy began as a dancer and went on to refine her use of movement and gesture in silent films where body and face had to express every emotion.

It is startling and even sad that such outstanding performers and comediennes as Myrna Loy, Irene Dunne, Jean Arthur and Carole Lombard were never honored by their industry with an Academy Award. Their sort of polished comedy technique and superior playing are unappreciated accomplishments when the awards are handed out. In the entire history of motion pictures, only Claudette Colbert (in *It Happened One Night*) and Judy Holliday (in *Born Yesterday*) achieved this honor. Marlene Dietrich ironically pointed out that there are sure-fire roles for an Academy Award: people afflicted with mental disturbances, drunkenness, blindness, deafness or insanity. And biblical characters or priests and nuns are usually sure of a nomination. True? Just look at the winners down through the years.

Politics was a lifelong interest of Loy's. After World War II she served for three and a half years as a member of the United States Commission for UNESCO, fought McCarthyism, and, while living in Washington with her fourth husband, Howland Sargeant, campaigned with Eleanor Roosevelt for Adlai Stevenson. Loy was praised on the floor of Congress by then Representative Mike Mansfield of Montana for her tireless work for the United Nations. Since 1960 she has been an active member of the National Committee Against Discrimination in Housing ("President Kennedy steered me into that!").

There was a retrospective of Loy's films at the Second Los Angeles International Film Institute in 1972, and another tribute to her by John Springer in New York at Town Hall in his "Legendary Ladies of the Movies" series. Loy, Bette Davis, Joan Crawford, Sylvia Sidney and Lana Turner each had an evening with memorable film clips from their long and varied careers; Loy's ranged from her oriental apprenticeship through her years as the quintessential American wife, to her later roles as a character actress of wide range. Here are Loy and John Springer, March 18, 1973, at her Town Hall tribute (left).

A star in every decade since the 1920's, Loy has just finished two films at this writing and started rehearsals for another play. In Hollywood, she and Pat O'Brien played the parents of Burt Reynolds in *The End,* and from there she flew to Vancouver to make a picture for television on "ants who have decided that they've had enough of that stuff we've been spraying on them."

Commenting on the current scene in Hollywood, she said, "Getting older is a very difficult thing in this country. In England, it's different; there you play character roles after you cease being radiantly beautiful. Here, most of the roles for older women are monsters. I don't know why they do that.

"And there is an unfortunate feeling that when you stop being a star and you play lesser roles that you are no longer a success. Some actors refuse to play them— they want their names above the title. I gave that up long ago."

For the past decade Loy has spent much of her time on the stage. She toured for two years in *Barefoot in the Park,* receiving Chicago's Sarah Siddons Award for her performance in that play. She toured again in *Dear Love,* based on Elizabeth Barrett Browning's letters. "We had great success with it on the road when we played small houses like the Alley Theater in Houston where the audience is attuned to that sort of play. I feel badly that there is not the proper theater to bring it to New York."

Just after her Town Hall tribute she made her Broadway debut in *The Women,* in March 1973, the cast of which also included Alexis Smith, Kim Hunter and Rhonda Fleming. Loy remains active and popular, one of New York's most sought-after women. She usually can be seen at any new play and if you wonder, "Isn't that Myrna Loy?" it probably is!

Loy is one of the very few—almost the only one who comes to mind—who at one time or another did not copy the look of other stars. During her lengthy career, she never tried on the Garbo or Crawford look, for example, as did most of her contemporaries, but always kept her own individuality and remained Myrna Loy.

Myrna Loy with Mrs. Jackie Onassis at the April in Paris Ball in 1976. Credit: New York *Post*

Myrna Loy with the author at the funeral of their friend of many years, Joan Crawford, in May 1977

RÉSUMÉ

CAROLE LOMBARD

Luminous and irrepressible Carole Lombard remains one of the great treasures from the films of the 30's and early 40's. During those years, she personified the ultimate All-American Girl; not only was she elegantly beautiful, bright and glamorous, but she also was honest, down-to-earth and a good sport. It was an irresistible combination. Her name inevitably appears on almost everyone's list of prominent Hollywood comediennes. Properly so! And it is a gauge of Lombard's place in film history that, since her death, she has become a criterion by which female comedic actresses are measured.

For Lombard was one of that rare genre who could be not only funny but fun. Early in her career, she received valuable training under the expert tutelage of Mack Sennett, whose wild and woolly comedies provided a marvelous apprenticeship. After sound arrived and dialogue was added to the visual, one of her greatest assets was her distinctive and well-modulated voice. It could go from a deep growl to a high, hysterical laugh without missing a beat. And her hands and body were graceful and agile unlike some of her contemporaries who depended primarily on their voices to express emotion.

In the 30's, Hollywood perfected what came to be known as "screwball comedy." Here, Lombard was at her peak! After a remarkably rapid rise to stardom, she became the highest-paid star in Hollywood in 1937, earning an unprecedented salary of $465,000 that year. By then, she also was the undisputed Queen of Comedy. Following the pattern for beautiful comediennes originated in silent pictures by Gloria Swanson, Bebe Daniels and Constance Talmadge, Lombard then added her own zany madness.

A small handful, Jean Arthur, Irene Dunne and Myrna Loy, also were able to gracefully juggle comedy and drama, but no one surpassed Lombard. For her deft performance in *My Man Godfrey,* she was nominated for an Academy Award as best actress but lost to Luise Rainer in *The Great Ziegfeld.* It's so strange: Hollywood would recognize a great comedy performance by nomination but not honor it with an award. This is evidenced by Irene Dunne's *Theodora Runs Wild* and *The Awful Truth;* Jean Arthur's *The More the Merrier;* Garbo's *Ninotchka;* Barbara Stanwyck's *Ball of Fire;* Rosalind Russell's *My Sister Eileen* and *Auntie Mame;* and the more recent *Pillow Talk* with Doris Day. All lost!

Born October 6, 1908, in Fort Wayne, Indiana, she was named Jane Alice Peters. Her parents were Elizabeth Knight and Frederic S. Peters; her brothers, Frederic Jr. and Stuart. In August 1914 her mother, called "Bess," brought her three children to Los Angeles for an extended vacation that turned into a permanent stay.

Jane Peters made her film debut at twelve, playing a very small role as a tomboy in *A Perfect Crime,* a film directed by a neighbor, film pioneer Allan Dwan, who had observed the future star playing outside her home. But her real career began at age sixteen when she signed her first film contract with Fox studios in October 1924. It was common practice in those days for studios to place teen-age girls under stock contracts for grooming as potential leading ladies to male stars. Myrna Loy, Jean Arthur, Janet Gaynor and Mary Astor were among those who started their careers in that fashion about the same time.

With absolutely no experience, Lombard was rushed prematurely into leading-lady roles opposite Edmund Lowe and Buck Jones, the cowboy star. The studio, realizing its mistake, then put her in lesser roles to gain experience. She had begun work on her sixth film when her face was scarred in an automobile accident. She and Heinie Cooper, a dancing companion from a prominent Los Angeles family, were returning from a football game in Cooper's Bugatti roadster one foggy night when the accident occurred. It shattered the windshield, which cut a long, deep gash across Lombard's left cheek. Plastic surgery preserved the face but left a scar. So Fox dropped her—a discouraging experience for the seventeen-year-old Lombard.

She was determined to proceed, however, and after having plastic surgery she studied camera lighting and the right angles to camouflage the scar. Much later in her career, Ted Tetzlaff, the gifted cameraman who photographed ten Lombard films, was encouraged by her to emphasize her bone structure and hollow cheeks, qualities which she admired in Dietrich and copied from her. Expert cinematographer Harry Stradling said, "She knew as much about the tricks of the trade as I do. In closeup work, I wanted to cover her scar simply by focusing the lights on her face so that it would seem to blend with her cheek. She told me that a diffusing light would do the same job better. And she was right." Like Crawford, Garbo, Dietrich and Hepburn, Lombard had the intelligence to learn every factor of her trade which would improve her performance and appearance, educating herself in all the technical aspects of film-making.

Soon after her recovery from the accident, Lombard joined an amateur theater group in Hollywood to further her acting experience. Her pal, Sally Eilers, then told her of a vacancy in Mack Sennett's stock company assembly of "bathing beauties."

She applied and got the job, signing with Sennett in 1927. There she chased policemen, threw pies, squirted hoses and galloped about in bathing suits for a year and a half while she learned the slapstick, abandon and timing demanded by silent pictures. All these skills were to prove invaluable later. While with that studio she also met Madalyne Fields, who was destined to become her best friend, secretary and life-long companion.

Offscreen, Carole Lombard was warm, direct and honest, with irrepressible good humor. Despite her chic, beautiful exterior, she remained refreshingly earthy, a pithy lady who made friends of everyone who knew her. As a star, she was bright, articulate and knowledgeable, one who excelled in both comedy and melodrama. She stood among those at the very top of her profession until her untimely death on January 6, 1942. Her greatest popularity stemmed from her brilliant comedy performances in such farces as *Twentieth Century, Hands Across the Table, My Man Godfrey* and *True Confession.* In these films her mastery of the mocking wisecrack and talent for comedy so endeared her to audiences that they placed her at the top of the wacky genre, and *Life* magazine dubbed her the "Duse of Daffy Comedy."

Lombard also had a penchant for sophisticated foolery but she wasn't given adequate opportunity to use her blossoming talent for high comedy. I suspect that she could have been equally adept indulging in the exquisite badinage of a Philip Barry or Frederick Lonsdale. Her 1933 film, *Brief Moment,* written by S. N. Behrman, and moments in *Fast and Loose, Man of the World* and *Ladies' Man* evidenced her ease with the butterfly touch. (And imagine the mature Lombard as Auntie Mame! Chic, sophisticated, lovable and loving, tough but vulnerable, she really would have been perfectly cast.) Such dramas as *No Man of Her Own, In Name Only, Vigil in the Night* and *They Knew What They Wanted* proved her effectiveness as a dramatic actress, but her fans chiefly enjoyed her irreverent high spirits and hoydenish clowning, identifying most strongly with her in films in which she displayed these qualities.

In 1936, Barbara Stanwyck, another eminent star of the period, said that she considered Lombard "Hollywood's most interesting person because she is so alive, modern, frank and natural." More than forty years later, contemporary film audiences are still enjoying these same qualities. This volume will dwell on her Fabulous Face while paying tribute to her lovable humanness, her acting ability and her svelte beauty, with the hope that these rare photographs will help readers gain a deeper insight into the person and personality of Carole Lombard.

"As a child, I had a round face, wore my hair in a Dutch bob and was fat. I was a tomboy, a fighter, and I loved the movies—especially the serials on Saturday afternoon. I adored Pearl White; I always think of her in that black velvet tam, that short jacket and her flowing tie. What thrills!

"Whenever I have to go through some fast scenes, I think of doing a Pearl White." (Pearl White was the Queen of the Serials and the star of *The Perils of Pauline.*)

"I entered pictures when I was fifteen . . . applied to the Fox Studio and, unfortunately, was given the leading role opposite Edmund Lowe in *Marriage in Transit.* I was terrible—worse than that, if possible. At the end of a year, they threw me out. They should have done it before!

"My best tutor was Mack Sennett—a wonderful teacher. His knowledge of comedy, of timing, use of pantomime, the sudden change from comedy to tragedy or from laughter to tears . . . well, he had grasped the psychology of the human mind."
—Dorothy Woolridge, *Picture Play,* June 1934

"Sennett's was the most delightful madhouse imaginable! There was a lusty, rowdy freedom I've never encountered anywhere else. . . . Two years there gave me such a thorough background that I left fully prepared to face the world."
—Malcolm H. Oethinger, *Picture Play,* December 30

The Sennett stock company has been described as a "great gallery of grotesques," vaudevillians and circus clowns plus his "bathing beauties," the pretty girls he used for contrast. Sennett later recalled Lombard as "a scamp and a madcap." From him she learned timing, teamwork and every trick of visual comedy used in silent pictures.

"From Sennett, I went to Pathé [studios] where I changed my name from Carol Peters to Carol Lombard. When I was a little girl, I had changed my first name from Jane to Carol because I didn't like Jane. I took the name Lombard from a friend" (The family's neighbor and close friend, Harry Lombard).

At Pathé, 1928–29, she continued her apprenticeship, developing as a performer, personality and beauty. "I was learning. . . . In the easy camaraderie of a small studio, we all had a hand in the pie."
Lombard in *High Voltage* and *Big News,* 1929 (next page)

Lombard's scar from the 1925 accident, usually hidden by make-up, lighting and retouching, can be seen here, faint but evident.

For the next few years, Lombard continued experimenting with her looks, changing her makeup for mouth, eyes and eyebrows, and altering the color and style of her hair. These pages illustrate her endeavors as she searched for her own "look" (opposite page).

Lombard at Paramount and Bette Davis at Warner Bros. both tried on the Constance Bennett look. For a while the fan magazines were featuring stories and layouts on the three look-alikes.

Davis

Lombard

Bennett

In 1930 and 1931, Joan Crawford's heavy eye makeup was widely copied. Here Lombard experiments with it and adds her own black eyebrows. Fortunately she soon adopted a more natural and becoming look, but this experiment was part of her metamorphosis.

Lombard in the 1930 Buddy Rogers film, *Safety in Numbers*. Surrounding Rogers are: (clockwise from top left) Virginia Bruce, Lombard, Kathryn Crawford and Josephine Dunn. Lombard made such a vivid impression in this movie with her poised performance and smashing appearance that Paramount studios signed her to a long-term contract and added an *e* to her first name.

With Fredric March in *The Eagle and the Hawk*

Lombard with Chester Morris in *Sinners in the Sun,* 1932

Dietrich   1931

Lombard made two films, *Man of the World* and *Ladies' Man*, in 1931 with William Powell. They were married on June 26 of that year, but the marriage lasted only until August 18, 1933. Louella Parsons, then Hollywood's leading columnist—who always took "pride in being the first to announce" anything, no matter how trivial—headlined her column during 1933 with an unusual amount of divorces for even that town. When she breathlessly announced the impending divorces of both Mary Pickford and Douglas Fairbanks, Sr., and of Lombard and Powell within one week, some wag dubbed her "Love's Undertaker."

Lombard's ability to wear striking clothes with flair and authority resulted in her being dubbed a "best-dressed woman" in fashion columns, while at the same time her studio's publicity department billed her as "The Orchid Lady." Seen here with her constant companion after her divorce, singer Russ Columbo. "We had been going together for eight months, and the very weekend he was killed he had planned to join his mother and me at my mountain cabin."

With Powell (opposite top), Columbo (opposite left) and Fredric March (right)

Probably the major influence in the evolution of Lombard's eventual look was Marlene Dietrich. Copying the Dietrich style of overhead lighting, Lombard found that it emphasized her excellent bone structure, so she retained it.

1936

Ascent and descent in Hollywood could be unbelievably swift: John Barrymore was still a prominent personality in the movie capital in 1934 when he starred in *Twentieth Century* with Lombard as his leading lady. After finishing the picture, Lombard said, "A picture with Barrymore is wild and delicious . . . experience with a capital E! You start in as one person and emerge quite another," which is exactly what happened to her. Barrymore taught her to relax and abandon herself in the part of Lily Garland, a tempestuous stage actress. She "emerged" from this film a Star and never forgot her indebtedness to Barrymore, who praised her as "probably the greatest actress I've ever worked with" when the movie was completed. In describing her a few years later he eliminated the word "probably."

By the time *True Confession* was filmed in 1937, three short years later, Barrymore was a perceptibly fallen star, and Lombard had become the biggest figure on the Paramount lot. She insisted that his role be enlarged with co-star billing although he was playing only a supporting role to her and Fred MacMurray. Lombard's generous gesture and Barrymore's brilliant performance resulted in a resurgence of prestige and popularity for him despite the fact that years of dissipation had obviously taken their toll. He died in 1942, a caricature of his former self.

1931

1933

1935

With Barrymore
in *True Confes-
sion*

Lombard's metamorphosis from 1930 to 1935 is most evident in these two portraits; the early façade of sophistication matured into the authentic article.

When Baron George Hoyningen-Huene, the distinguished Russian photographer for *Vanity Fair* and *Vogue,* traveled to Hollywood in 1934 to make portraits of its beautiful women, Lombard was on the threshold of her great success. His comments were: "Carole Lombard is a most unusual woman who could be a very important actress if she had the chance. I am told she more nearly displays her possibilities in *Twentieth Century* than in anything she has done. Otherwise, she has played falsely sophisticated women but they are not herself. She is energetic, full of good will and genuine gaiety, and she has intelligence of a high order plus imagination.

"Miss Lombard bounds around her dressing room in an excess of good animal spirits. It was an agreeable surprise to find her so vivacious! She has great chic, a real feeling for fashion, and an interesting face with a fine sculptural forehead. She had so much fun posing that two hours seemed like ten minutes."

Lombard was usually the center of any group; her spontaneous rapport with everyone made her so immediately appealing that people naturally gravitated to her. Her set, her dressing room, her table in the studio commissary were always crowded with friends and fellow performers. As with Myrna Loy, it's difficult to find anyone who didn't like her. The affection she aroused was genuine, deep and lasting.

CAROLE LOMBARD

Lombard and Fred MacMurray in *Hands Across the Table* (above), 1935. Their personalities and performances blended beautifully. His blossoming talent for comedy was a perfect foil for her beauty and contagious high spirits, making them so popular with movie audiences that Paramount starred them in three subsequent films: *The Princess Comes Across,* 1936, *Swing High, Swing Low,* 1937, and *True Confession,* 1937.

Lombard is seen here (top right) with Travis Banton, who designed all her clothes at Paramount, and Mary O'Brien, her fitter, as a style conference takes place for *The Princess Comes Across*. Said Banton, "Carole Lombard has great natural chic! She wears clothes beautifully and possesses the rare knack of being able to put them on and forget about them."

Lombard and George Raft, seen here in *Bolero,* in which they danced to Maurice Ravel's famous composition. Like Davis, Loy and Del Rio, Lombard loved dancing and had studied it as a child.

During her teens Lombard was part of a group that vied in Charleston contests at Wednesday night dances at the Montmartre and Friday nights at the Coconut Grove. Joan Crawford, newly arrived from a New York chorus line, and Lombard's local pals, Sally Blane, Helen Twelvetrees, Doris Dawson and Carmen Pantages, were prominent contestants in these competitions. Later, Lombard's dancing experience was to prove a great asset when she filmed *Bolero* and *Rumba* with George Raft.

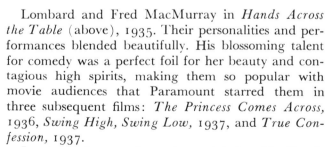

CAROLE LOMBARD
Paramount Pictures

In 1935, Lombard posed in front of an earlier 1931 portrait, illustrating the subtle changes that five years had wrought in her appearance: fuller mouth, more natural eyebrows and a softer, darker shade of hair.

By 1937, Lombard had become Hollywood's highest-paid star, earning almost half a million dollars, an astounding salary achievement in that day. With such outstanding 1936 successes as *The Princess Comes Across* and *My Man Godfrey,* for which she received an Academy Award nomination, she truly became the queen of screwball comedy. The zenith of her success came in 1937 with three terrific hits, *Swing High, Swing Low; True Confession;* and *Nothing Sacred.*

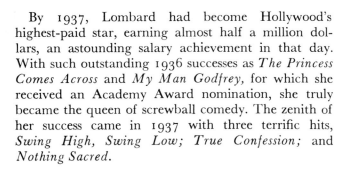

THE MEN IN HER LIFE

First husband, William Powell

Russ Columbo

Travis Banton, her designer and fashion mentor

Clark Gable, her second husband

Gable and Lombard first met when they filmed *No Man of Her Own* in 1932. At the time, Carole was married to William Powell, and Clark to Ria Langham. Several years later they met again and began a torrid romance that culminated in their marriage on May 29, 1939.

As Mrs. Clark Gable, Lombard adapted her life style to his, and the former glamour girl who had loved parties now pursued an active outdoor life, becoming an ardent sportswoman who accompanied Gable on hunting trips. She is seen here with "her own plane" and ready for skeet shooting on the San Fernando Valley ranch she and Gable shared.

HAIR STYLES

CAROLE LOMBARD

LEADING MEN

With George Raft

During her climb to stardom Lombard was leading lady to Warner Baxter, Cary Grant and Fredric March, John Barrymore, in addition to William Boyd, Robert Armstrong, Buddy Rogers, William Powell, Gary Cooper, Pat O'Brien, Clark Gable, Gene Raymond, Charles Laughton and Bing Crosby.

After attaining stardom, she appeared with: George Raft in *Bolero* and *Rumba*, Cesar Romero in *Love Before Breakfast*, Fred MacMurray in *The Princess Comes Across*, William Powell in *My Man Godfrey*, Fredric March in *Nothing Sacred* and Robert Montgomery in *Mr. and Mrs. Smith*.

She also had co-starring roles with Fernand Gravet in *Fools for Scandal*, Cary Grant in *In Name Only*, Brian Aherne in *Vigil in the Night*, Charles Laughton in *They Knew What They Wanted*, and her last film, *To Be or Not to Be* with Jack Benny.

With Warner Baxter

With John Barrymore

With Cary Grant and Fredric March

With Cesar Romero

With Fred MacMurray

With William Powell

With Fredric March

With Robert Montgomery

In 1937, Lombard posed for a portrait painted by Azadia Newman, the wife of director Rouben Mamoulian. The painting was to be one of a series of color inserts for a swanky new magazine called *Cinema Arts* (the *Vanity Fair* of movie magazines). Despite its beauty and quality, the magazine lasted for only three issues; its fifty-cent price was just too expensive for a Depression-oriented audience accustomed to paying ten cents for its favorite magazine. So the portrait was never published and is shown here for the first time.

Fearing that audiences might tire of seeing her only in comedies, Lombard decided to vary her film roles by switching to drama. In 1939 she appeared with Jimmy Stewart in *Made for Each Other* and in *In Name Only,* which reunited her with two old friends and fellow players from her Paramount days, Cary Grant and Kay Francis. Box office responses were favorable, so Lombard continued her drama phase with *Vigil in the Night,* about which *Motion Picture Herald* commented, ". . . splendidly produced and inescapably effective. Carole Lombard gives a command-

ing portrayal of the austerely fervent nurse." In the March 11, 1977, issue of the New York *Times,* Pandro S. Berman, who produced both *In Name Only* and *Vigil in the Night,* was interviewed about his upcoming Academy Award, the Irving Thalberg Award. Speaking of some of the many stars he had worked with during Hollywood's golden years, he recalled, "I'd say Carole Lombard was the nicest girl I made pictures with!"

After co-starring with Charles Laughton in the 1940's version of *They Knew What They Wanted,* a 1920's play by Sidney Howard, which had been made as a silent picture by Pola Negri and again as an early talkie by Vilma Banky and Edward G. Robinson, to the delight of her fans, Lombard then resumed her comedy career with Robert Montgomery in *Mr. and Mrs. Smith.*

Lombard's directness and honesty, combined with her natural exuberant spirits, endeared her to her co-workers, while the comprehension and technical knowledge she brought to her performances made her one of their most favorite actresses. She was filmdom's best pal.

When the Studios ran Hollywood, it was graced with the greatest number of superior "supporting players" ever assembled. Many had been former stars of the stage and all contributed immeasurably to the overall prestige and distinction of any films in which they appeared. Like all her contemporaries, Lombard benefited from working with such performers as Frank Morgan, Ilka Chase, Guy Kibbee, Lilyan Tashman, Paul Lukas, Alison Skipworth, Ward Bond, Louise Closser Hale, C. Aubrey Smith, Elizabeth Patterson, Beryl Mercer, Jack Oakie, Walter Connolly, Sir Guy Standing, Zasu Pitts, Mischa Auer, Eugene Pallette, Alan Mowbray, Charles Butterworth, Charles Winninger, Anthony Quinn, Una Merkel, Charles Coburn, Lucille Watson, Lionel Atwill, Akim Tamiroff and William Demarest. What a pleasure it is today to watch old films in which these performers appeared and added their professional magic!

Hollywood and, indeed, the entire world was stunned at Carole Lombard's sudden death on January 16, 1942. It was a particularly poignant demise: she had been on a national bond-selling tour at the behest of President Roosevelt, a much-publicized trip during which Lombard sold over two million dollars' worth of bonds and achieved a pronounced personal triumph, charming audiences wherever she appeared. Her mother accompanied her on the journey and was with her on the plane returning to Hollywood when it veered off course and crashed into the side of a mountain near Las Vegas, instantly killing everyone aboard.

Lombard with her mother, Mrs. Bessie Peters (above), in 1932 shortly after Carole joined Paramount Pictures, and again in 1942. The two always were very close and Mrs. Peters was with Lombard on that fatal plane trip. In one of the very last pictures ever taken during the bond rally tour, they are shown in Chicago on January 15 as they changed trains en route to the War Defense Bond Rally at Indianapolis.

There was national mourning for the vibrant young woman who died so tragically while performing a patriotic job for her country. She was saluted as a heroine. Governor Henry Schricker of Indiana, Carole's home state, named its Navy air squadron "The Lombardians," and in June that same year, Irene Dunne christened a Liberty ship *Carole Lombard* in her honor.

The greatest loss, of course, was to Lombard's own world of motion pictures, where she was unrivaled as a performer and inimitable as a person. From time to time since her death there has appeared "another Carole Lombard" but, with the possible exception of the also short-lived Kay Kendall (who, for all her talent and beauty, wasn't really another Lombard), no one has come near to matching her unique qualities. She remains sorely missed, but her deftness as a comedienne and her individuality as an actress endure in her films so that generation after generation can continue to enjoy Carole Lombard.

FASHION

One of Lombard's earliest fashion influences was Peggy Hopkins Joyce, the much-married New York show girl. Miss Joyce, blonde and beautiful, was famous for her diamonds, chic clothes and many love affairs, all of which she annotated in her autobiography, *Men, Marriage, and Me*. In the mid-20's she came to Hollywood with much fanfare to star in a silent film, *The Skyrocket,* and was dubbed "The Circe of the Cinema." The teen-aged Lombard observed her at a tea dance at the Coconut Grove. Impressed by Joyce's New York glamour and sophisticated simplicity, a striking contrast to the then prevailing penchant in Hollywood for ruffles and bows, Lombard chose her as a model for her own appearance and began dressing in simple black gowns ornamented occasionally by a strand of pearls or a severe piece of jewelry. Such attire made her stand out among the other young ingenues and led to her first film contract.

Next on Lombard's fashion horizon was Lilyan Tashman, another chic blonde clotheshorse, who, like Joyce, was an alumna of the *Ziegfeld Follies*. Tashman, the wife of actor Edmund Lowe, was an excellent comedienne, but her chief (and self-promoted) claim to fame was her ability to wear striking, innovative clothes with style and authority. She properly was known as one of Hollywood's best-dressed women, competing for that title with such contemporaries as Gloria Swanson, Constance Bennett and Kay Francis. Lombard learned also from her.

In late 1929, Constance Bennett returned to Hollywood fresh from five years of living abroad as the wealthy and internationally social Mrs. Philip Plant. Bennett had the ultimate look and style to which Lombard aspired, a continental chic that transcended even the elegance of Tashman.

Tashman   Lombard   Bennett

To the youthful Lombard, who then had never been farther east than her native Indiana, these three women represented exactly what she'd like to become —and ultimately did!

In 1933, by which time Lombard was a personality and fashion-setter to be reckoned with, Peggy Hopkins Joyce returned to Hollywood under contract, coincidentally, to Lombard's studio, Paramount. More mature, she was still beautiful and chic but the screen now had numerous exponents of blonde sophistication: Marlene Dietrich, Tallulah Bankhead, Ann

Harding, Ina Claire and Lombard herself. Joyce's film appearance in *International House* with, of all people, W. C. Fields, made only a slight impression on the movie-goers of that era. Lilyan Tashman died in 1934 and Constance Bennett's reign as a Top Star was soon over, although her career continued. By 1936, Lombard had created her very own look and style, and outdistanced all the others.

Carole Lombard was one of the best dressed of all the Hollywood stars, with Travis Banton the guiding force in this undertaking. "She was just a tootsie

when she came to Paramount but he saw things in her even she didn't know she had. His clothes transformed her!" commented a contemporary. Banton himself said, "Throw a bolt of material at Carole and any way it hits her she'll look great." He loved her long, slim lines, describing her as "a greyhound or an Arabian horse." When Lombard switched from comedy to drama, his clothes were an important aid in helping her gain stature as a serious actress; straight lines and stark simplicity replaced the more elaborate clothes he once had designed for her.

All Lombard's designers—Banton, Robert Kalloch, Walter Plunkett and Irene—appreciated her perfect figure, and there is total evidence of it in photographs throughout this section. Lombard had a very strong personality that allowed her to wear dramatic clothes easily while giving less inspired costumes some of the dash she possessed in such abundance. The early fashion pictures are a revelation, showing how quickly her clothes changed from chorine to soignée.

She was elegant off screen as well as on: The Banton evening gowns she wore with William Powell and Russ Columbo were structurally simple, allowing the beads and flamboyant prints to stand on their own. She adored Banton's clothes and he adored designing for her. Lombard and Marlene Dietrich were his special favorites and some of his loveliest ideas showed up on both of them: the scarfed helmet worn by Dietrich in *Desire* and, again, by Lombard in *The Princess*

Comes Across; also the wreath of furs at the neck of two costumes shown in the Résumé. Banton did most of her clothes (she demanded and got him even for pictures she made on loanout from Paramount) until 1937. Banton was drinking heavily by then, and when Lombard left Paramount, Irene largely took over.

In Irene's clothes, Lombard looked more mature, and more severe, due less to the fact that she was approaching thirty than that the fashion look was

changing from the glamour and beauty of the 30's to the drama and wartime style of the 40's. But there were exceptions, especially the shimmeringly lovely dress by Irene worn by Lombard at the pre-mière of *Gone With the Wind*. (See pg. 131.)

Edith Head, long Hollywood's premier designer, said of Lombard, "Her clothes always looked as if they belonged to her . . . some girls never learn to wear elegance naturally, but it seemed that Carole had always known how . . . She could turn just about anything, even a dress fitting, into some kind of a party. Great care went into those clothes and a fitting was sure to be a tedious thing, requiring four or five hours, sometimes eight or ten, at a time. Carole, though, was patience itself."

RÉSUMÉ

BETTE DAVIS

For all of her adult life, Bette Davis has been a hard-working, professional actress, the deserved recipient of some of the highest acclaim—and deepest criticism—ever received by any motion picture star.

There are those who consider her "The First Lady of the Screen," an opinion with which various film critics and historians concurred, particularly during those vintage years when she appeared in such a dazzling succession of extraordinarily fine films. That peak period began in 1938 with *Jezebel,* and her subsequent pictures through 1945 were well-crafted vehicles with top co-stars and supporting casts, designed to display her at her best.

A devastating personality, inimitable face and husky bottled-in-brine voice combined with a multifaceted electricity made her one of filmdom's reigning box office queens. She wasn't everyone's cup of tea; it has been said of her, "She's a person you either love or hate!" But I'm not sure that's necessarily true, or even fair. She is far too complex to be so easily evaluated.

Passionately involved in every aspect of her career, Bette Davis contributed some major and distinguished screen performances—as well as some blatantly bad ones. Her enormous talent could get out of hand when she lacked a firm director to guide her. No performer has a perfect batting average, but in Davis' case an increasing tendency to overact contributed to her decline; she became too mannered, a highly perfected technician whose excesses commanded attention but not admiration. As *Time* magazine said of one performance, "Her acting, as always, isn't really acting, it's shameful showing off. But just try to look away!"

Whether or not one judges Davis or any of her cinema contemporaries—Hepburn, Garbo, Crawford, Stanwyck, et al.—as genuinely great actresses, it must be acknowledged that they merit the overworked designation Superstar in every sense of the word. Stars of their magnitude are increasingly rare today. And that very word "superstar" has come close to having no real meaning with its constant application to short-lived embryonic singers and various rock groups.

But when the lengthy career and achievements of a Bette Davis are considered, the term has genuine meaning and real impact, for Davis is one of the most honored and commemorated women in the acting profession. She has had a career filled with triumph and failure . . . success and frustration. Eight times she was nominated for an Academy Award as Best Actress but won it only twice. She was elected the first woman president of the Academy of Motion Picture Arts and Sciences in 1942 but resigned over a difference of opinion about her true function in that role. In 1973 she was honored as a Legendary Lady of the Screen at Town Hall in New York, and in April 1977 she received the Life Achievement Award of the American Film Institute for her major contributions to the motion picture industry.

This chapter's primary focus, however, is not on the illustrious career of Bette Davis but rather on her face, its evolution and metamorphosis. It's a face that has undergone multiple changes, running the gamut from pale, reserved ingenue, through saucy, bleached blonde to the unique face instantly recognizable the world over. On a number of occasions in recent years, Davis has confided that she used to hate her looks: "I have never been terribly fond of my appearance," and "I always disliked enormously the way I looked." But now when she watches her old films she candidly admits, "I think I was the most beautiful human being I've ever seen," and laughs at her change of attitude.

Once her apprenticeship at Warner Bros. was completed and her box office value recognized, the studio did everything possible to glamorize her appearance as befitted the Queen of the lot. But Davis did not allow herself to get trapped into the prevailing mode of playing each role with the current glamour-girl look. When Hollywood persisted in having that "utter perfection" for all stars, of which I wrote earlier, a look sometimes totally inconsistent with the character being played, Davis fought for "realism," resisting the fashion of looking beautiful and immaculate whether sweating over a hot stove or waking from a deep sleep or dying from some dread disease. With a passion for detail, she insisted that the authenticity and integrity of her portrayal be maintained with proper makeup, accurate hair styles and appropriate clothes for the period. However, her ideas of "realism" and "appropriate" were not always shared by her directors and co-workers, and she often has been accused by the critics of "piling it on" too heavily in makeup and performance in such films as *Mr. Skeffington, In This Our Life, Beyond the Forest, What Ever Happened to*

Baby Jane? and others. "From beginning to end, there is not a life-like inflection, a plausible reaction . . ." reads one review. No, subtlety is a word not associated with Davis and the "realism" she espoused became a highly debatable definition. But close attention to every detail in the delineation of a character did become a Davis trademark, a part of her legend.

Also part of that legend are her hot temper, strong will and sharp tongue. Stories of her dictatorial behavior are legion: "Surely nobody but a mother could have loved Bette Davis at the height of her career," commented Brian Aherne in his autobiography, *A Proper Job,* in which he referred to some great women stars as "Monsters." Asked about her alleged temperament, Davis replied, "I was not brought up as a woman to be that way; I had to learn to be tough. But this is a business and you must fight for what you believe in." She was very frank in her autobiography, *The Lonely Life:* "I will never deny that I was on occasion insufferably rude and ill-mannered in the cultivation and preservation of my career. I had no time for pleasantries. I said what was on my mind and it wasn't always printable."

Apparently time has brought little mellowness. I've talked with a number of people who have known and worked with her during her long career and the reactions ranged from well disposed to downright hostile. Some refused to discuss her at all while others insisted on anonymity. Comments on Davis tend to be as extravagant as the lady herself.

One of her biggest boosters is director Robert Aldrich (*What Ever Happened to Baby Jane?* and *Hush . . . Hush, Sweet Charlotte*). In an interview with Guy Flatley in the New York *Times* of February 4, 1977, Aldrich said, "In terms of talent and the special knowledge she has of the medium, Bette is the greatest single talent in the history of film—an incredibly gifted lady who uses her extraordinary art with unfailing intelligence. She is head and shoulders above the others who follow her profession." Certainly no performer could ask for higher praise.

On the other side of the ledger, asking not to be identified, a well-known performer who has known her for years talked very candidly: "It could be marvelous working with Bette . . . and it could be absolute hell. Everything depended on her mood at the time; when she was in a good mood, the cast and crew would relax and filming went smoothly. But when she started her famous tirades—watch out! At such times, her behavior was so counterproductive that the picture and everyone connected with it suffered accordingly. She seemed to thrive on conflict, to want to create turmoil, and when this sort of thing occurred, she was the greatest bitch I've ever known! [In a recent interview, Davis declared, "You know, a star can wreck a set . . . funnily enough, with all my reputation, I never blew a set. Never!" Obviously, others disagree.]

"Of course, there were times when her impatience was certainly justified—unnecessarily long delays and frustrating incompetence—but they didn't explain those occasions when she just seemed to go out of her way to be rude and disagreeable. During several such occurrences I simply said, 'Let me know when it's over' and withdrew to my dressing room.

"On the other hand, she *could* be so marvelous to work with and give you so much while you were performing with her that you had that rare satisfaction you can only get working with a great pro. We used to see each other socially once in a while but that, too, became too fraught with suspense. Her moods changed as swiftly and unexpectedly at dinner as they had on the set, so you never knew what to expect. Finally I gave up seeing her. I suppose I still like her in a way—certainly I respect her great ability. I do wish she were a more relaxed person; it would make it so much easier for everyone if she could be happier."

Another friend said pretty much the same thing and added, "Bette is really unable, for any great length of time, to conceal the fact that she honestly considers herself God's greatest gift to screen acting. She believes that to be a simple fact of life. Oh, she can be disarmingly candid and funny about herself for a short while—sometimes seem even modest. But soon that overwhelming ego of hers starts rising to the surface again."

Davis has written frankly about herself and her career in her autobiography, *The Lonely Life* (1962), and in the more recent *Mother Goddam* (1974). The recollections of a star, to begin with, are inclined to be a fanciful and ingenious amalgam of fact, fantasy and fiction. Memory can play strange tricks, and actresses do not write or tape their memoirs under oath; sometimes verifiable facts and documentary evidence seem of less interest to them than their own emotional reactions to the events and people that helped shape their careers. Thus their autobiographies are not only revisionist, they become history manqué. All recollections tend to be colored by personal viewpoint so that the more prosaic matters of truth and fact are left to less involved writers and plodding researchers. And let the young or inexperienced researcher beware accepting as fact all he may find in the morgue, for reality and invention lie side by side there.

Still Hollywood *does* have a viable and visible history. Seeking the facts, one can see old films and evaluate them, and search yesterday's reputable newspapers and periodicals to arrive at a reasonable conclusion.

An example: one often reads that Cary Grant was "discovered" by Mae West, a bit of fiction invented by the lady herself. In her "autobiography," a misnomer if ever there was one, that queen of fantasy writes that she "discovered Cary Grant walking along the studio street" at Paramount, and, without even meeting him said, "He'll do for my leading man." In her version, the producers protested, "But he hasn't made a picture yet. Only tests." But she persisted, so the inexperienced newcomer was cast opposite her in *She Done Him Wrong!* Since few people, apparently, have ever checked out this charming fable, the legend endures.

But what are the facts? Well, at the time that Miss West made her big "discovery" of the allegedly untried Cary Grant, he had been on the Paramount lot for over two years (!) and had made eight films playing opposite such even then renowned stars as Marlene Dietrich, Nancy Carroll, Tallulah Bankhead, Sylvia Sidney, Carole Lombard and Lili Damita! Not at all the novice that West, to this day, continues to claim, he was a popular, fast-rising leading man who was considered a potential star. But because the West assertion is in print, in the morgue and in almost every biographical report on Cary Grant, the truth and reality of the eight previous films is forgotten, ignored or unreported.

Similarly, one's admiration for Bette Davis can become tinged with exasperation after reading her books and hearing her assert, time and again, such absurdities as "I never had a male co-star," "I carried my pictures alone: Warners didn't believe in wasting two big names in one film," "I didn't have many good directors," and "I was the first woman to pay alimony." One can get the impression that her historical horizon is bounded on the north, south, east and west by only Bette Davis.

While there is no wish nor endeavor to diminish the contribution of Bette Davis to the art of film (her indisputable place in screen history is too secure for that!), excessive and unquestioning praise tends to blur the truth. Davis is a very complex woman with many conflicting facets; when only a complimentary picture of her is presented it becomes an incomplete portrait. It is impossible for her to be dispassionate about herself or her career, so hyperbole and exaggeration are likely to emerge in any of *her* discussions about herself or her films. She is a highly opinionated woman whose comments are extremely definite and interesting, if not always accurate.

It must come as quite a surprise to the many Stars and distinguished players who have worked with Davis to learn from her that "My films—once I reached my peak—brought the public in without a co-star," or that "I didn't work with any big male stars; female stars didn't in those days. We were meant to carry the picture ourselves." As one recalls such popular and talented Stars as Errol Flynn, Henry Fonda, Charles Boyer, James Cagney, Leslie Howard, Paul Muni and Robert Montgomery, all of whom played opposite her in her "peak" years (1938–45), plus the co-starring contributions of Edward G. Robinson, Herbert Marshall, Brian Aherne, Joseph Cotten, George Brent, Paul Lukas, Miriam Hopkins and Olivia de Havilland, such patronizing

assertions that ignore the popularity and assistance of these players are startling and sad.

In writing and speaking of the many directors with whom she's worked through the years, Davis has repeatedly stated, "I didn't have many good directors." She speaks with admiration of a few: William Wyler, Edmund Goulding, Robert Aldrich, Richard Brooks and (occasionally) John Huston. Not mentioned is Joseph Mankiewicz, who directed *All About Eve,* which revived her faltering career and produced the performance most people consider her greatest; nor is John Cromwell, who directed *Of Human Bondage,* the film and performance that really launched her career. Dismissed are the valid accomplishments of such competent craftsmen and highly regarded men as Frank Capra, King Vidor, John M. Stahl, James Whale, William Wellman, Michael Curtiz, Anatole Litvak, John Farrow, Curtis Bernhardt and dozens of others.

Which directors does she consider great? Whom would she have liked to work with? It's hard to imagine her with those at Paramount; the mind boggles at the thought of Lubitsch, DeMille, Von Sternberg or Mitch Leisen teamed with Davis. At M-G-M, she would have worked with Cukor, Clarence Brown, Frank Borzage or Van Dyke. The combination of Davis and such disciplinarians as John Ford, George Stevens, Lewis Milestone or Howard Hawkes might have produced some interesting films. I can find no record of anyone asking her about these directors and the answers would be illuminating.

After reaching stardom, Davis (and also Katharine Hepburn) became deeply involved in every aspect of their pictures. Their forcefulness aroused mixed reactions from the men who directed them; some were intimidated, others were put off. But the strong who could cope with them were able to bring forth truly superb performances on their own terms, and such combinations (Wyler and Davis, Cukor and Hepburn) gave the screen some of its most brilliant films.

By ignoring time throughout much of her career, and playing roles of all ages, Davis did not have to worry too much about clinging to her youth, as did her contemporaries. In a sense, she was already ageless, so when maturity arrived she was able to slip into roles her own age with much more ease than those who tried to defy it. Some years earlier Claudette Colbert had told her, "Because you played older women before you had to, you'll never have to make the age bridge," a shrewd observation on that problem which, sooner or later, every actress must face.

In 1974, while rehearsing the stage production, *Miss Moffat,* a musical version of her film, *The Corn Is Green,* Davis commented, "I enjoy domesticity— living quietly at home. But after six months, my head gets stale. An older woman is extraordinarily lucky to have a profession. Josh Logan said, 'If you can give it up, then don't try it at all. But if you just can't help

doing something, then *do it!'* For me, acting is a wild profession, the toughest, toughest, toughest profession.

"I figure in four years I will have had it. It is silly at a certain age to continue. One is just not strong enough."

One can also hope that (when Davis' four-year plan is up) she doesn't retire. She is one of the very few left from that once great gallery of Stars of Hollywood's Golden Era. Joan Crawford, Miriam Hopkins, Kay Francis, Vivien Leigh, Jeanette MacDonald and Rosalind Russell are dead, and of the living, only Davis, Hepburn, Loy and Del Rio are still actively performing on stage and in films.

Indeed, we now have the promised combination of Hepburn and Davis to look forward to, if one screen is big enough to hold simultaneously two such *femmes formidables*.

The world-renowned actress who later would be described variously as "Popeye the Magnificent," "the little brown wren," "another Constance Bennett," "devouringly ambitious," "smoulderingly devastating," and "a craftsman who is something of a genius" began life as Ruth Elizabeth Davis in Lowell, Massachusetts, on April 5, 1908. The older daughter of Harlow M. Davis and Ruth Favor Davis, she was nicknamed "Betty." Then a friend of her mother's suggested the spelling "Bette" (as in Balzac's heroine in *La Cousine Bette*), "to set you apart, dear!" Her mother was known as "Ruthie" and her sister Barbara as "Bobbie"—Ruthie, Bette and Bobbie! Apparently Mrs. Davis liked the *E* sound of the three nicknames.

Her parents were divorced when she was eight and thereafter she and her sister were reared by their mother, who supplemented her income by working at a series of jobs: governess, housemother at a girls' boarding school, photographer and silhouette artist. (Her profile of Bette at age seventeen appears on page 195.) By the time Davis was twelve, she admits, she had become "stubborn and headstrong. . . . From that time on, I would brook no interference in anything I was determined to do."

Bette and her sister Barbara (Bobbie) at seventeen and sixteen (opposite, bottom center) and a portrait of Davis at twenty, when she was in stock at the Provincetown Playhouse in late 1928 (opposite, bottom right).

Earlier, she had been a student of Martha Graham (dancing was her first love), and had studied drama with John Murray Anderson in New York. From there, she went to a repertory company at the Lyceum Theater in Rochester, run by George Cukor, later one of Hollywood's most illustrious directors. After a few roles, Cukor let her go—a fact that Davis seems unwilling or unable to forget, since that dismissal always figures prominently in any biographical discussion. A few years ago Cukor said of the incident: "I'm constantly reading that Bette Davis was once fired by George Cukor. Sometimes she says it ironically—and sometimes with a kind of self-pity (and I'd really been awfully kind to her). Years later, our paths crossed and I said, 'Bette, for Christ's sake, stop talking about being fired once in Rochester. We've all been fired before and we'll all be fired again before we're dead!' She laughed—but not long after, I read another interview with her, and there it was again! I thought, she can't still be going on about this but, sure enough, she could."

After appearing on Broadway in *Broken Dishes* (1929) and the next year in *Solid South*, Davis was screen-tested by Universal Pictures and given a contract. She arrived in Hollywood on December 13, 1930. The studio appraised her screen potential: her ash-blonde hair photographed brown, her manner was shy and reticent. "Jean Harlow has nothing to worry about," was the sex-appeal evaluation.

She recently said of her cinematic beginning, "When many of us [stage actresses] got to Hollywood where there were all those absolutely fabulous-looking women in motion pictures, such glorious beauty as, say, Miss Harlow's, they didn't know what to do with us. We were the *shock* of the earth!"

Three 1931 portraits taken at Universal

After a year, Universal did not renew her contract, so Davis was prepared to return to New York. Just then George Arliss, the veteran character star, offered her a role in his film, *The Man Who Played God*, at Warner Bros. For the first time in Hollywood, real care was taken with her appearance by the makeup man, the hairdresser and the wardrobe department. Arliss made some suggestions—a lighter hue of hair and a slick coiffure. The improvement was striking and helped accentuate a resemblance to Constance Bennett. At that same time, a similar likeness to Bennett by Carole Lombard was noticed, and magazines and newspapers featured a triptych of the trio (as shown in the Lombard chapter of this book).

Her performance in the Arliss film (opposite, top) resulted in a long-term contract with Warner Bros. that was to last for eighteen years. Next she was cast in *So Big* with Barbara Stanwyck and George Brent (opposite, bottom), and simultaneously, in *The Rich Are Always with Us*, a Ruth Chatterton film in which Brent lit two cigarettes and handed one to Chatterton. Ten years later this "bit of business" was used again in *Now, Voyager* when Paul Henreid concurrently lit two cigarettes for Davis and himself. The second version attracted more attention, for some reason, and is still remembered by film buffs.

Recent revivals of many early Davis films have given today's audiences the opportunity to see and re-evaluate both the films and her performances. I found it an absorbing experience to watch these movies and observe her development first as a personality and then as an actress.

We watch yesterday's movies with different criteria, of course, so that some performances may seem better now than when seen originally, while others appear to have been over-applauded by contemporary critics. Writer Charles Affron observed that, in the Arliss and Ruth Chatterton films, "The syllables that fall to Davis stick in her throat," creating "verbal and visual rhythms that are both unsettling to the viewer and inappropriate to her supportive status."

The Davis face underwent chameleon-like changes during her career. The first look to be superimposed upon her was that of Constance Bennett: for a few films she took on the complete Bennett appearance—coiffure, makeup and style of dress, as did several other budding young actresses in the early 30's.

Constance Bennett was then one of the reigning stars of Hollywood. A trend-setter, she free-lanced among the top studios at a constantly escalating salary and had made three films for Warner Bros. As her fee per picture got more and more costly, it must have seemed providential to Warners to discover that they had under contract a new, much less expensive counterpart in young Bette Davis.

Constance Bennett

Bette Davis

At this point Louella Parsons, then the undisputed queen of Hollywood columnists (Hedda Hopper didn't begin writing her column until the very late 30's), took an interest in Davis and began touting her. Parsons' enthusiasm, however, did not extend to her appearance. "Bette Davis, young and with ability, has a great chance if she will put herself in the hands of a good makeup man," she wrote. Another time, she de-clared that she was delighted with Davis' continuing improvement as an actress but still deplored "her heavily beaded lashes and over-rouged mouth." In time, these distinguishing traits would become Davis trademarks.

A rare bathing-suit shot of Davis taken for publicity purposes (above)

Flattering makeup and hair styles, and beautiful clothes and backgrounds, embellished, of course, by expert lighting, were some of the devices employed by photographers to alter faces and achieve that "utter perfection" demanded by the studios. Minor and, sometimes, major miracles took place *during* and *after* a photo sitting. Expert retouchers airbrushed the faces for a faultless skin and reshaped any feature as desired! Mouths, teeth, noses, eyes and eyebrows could be "improved." That also included figures, which might be "too thin," "too fat," "too busty." Here are two examples of retouching in 1932 when Davis was a young twenty-four!

These portraits are a comprehensive illustration of the many changes in appearance that Davis experienced until she achieved the ultimate Bette Davis look so familiar to fans the world over.

These portraits were taken in 1932.

This set of four ranges from 1932 through 1940. Davis' mouth was reshaped and enlarged, her eyebrows first thinned, then thickened in diverse patterns. Her hair was colored in various shades and arranged in myriad styles. The studio strove to make a glamour girl of her and Davis was not unwilling. In her autobiography, she wrote, "Misses Crawford, Shearer and Dietrich were gorgeously glamorous. Part of me envied them, they were so beautiful."

It was common practice in Hollywood to copy each new trick of makeup, hair style or camera lighting. Any discovery that seemed to improve the appearance of one star was soon tested on others. So Davis, like everyone else, went through a series of experimental changes.

Of *Fashions of 1934* she wrote, "I was glamorized beyond recognition . . . the bossmen were trying to make me into a Greta Garbo," with a platinum wig dressed in the Garbo style, huge false eyelashes and a mouth copied from Joan Crawford. Someone must have liked this new look since it was retained for a subsequent film, *Jimmy the Gent* (top right).

Davis admired Garbo: "Her instinct, her mastery over the camera was pure witchcraft. I cannot analyze this woman's acting—I only know that no one else so effectively worked in front of a camera." She also held Katharine Hepburn in high esteem! ". . . that marvelous face! . . . I would have given anything to have looked like Katie Hepburn. I still would." The lipstick-slashed mouth favored by Hepburn with the upper lip painted in an unbroken semicircular shape was adapted also by Davis and added to her now familiar look of disdain and ennui.

In 1934, Davis got a role in a Leslie Howard film that altered the whole direction of her career. Her performance as the cheap Cockney waitress in Somerset Maugham's *Of Human Bondage* was the first real revelation of her genuine acting potential and enabled her to fight successfully for stronger, more appropriate parts from that time on. Author Jerry Vermilye recently gave this re-evaluation: "Seen today in light of more subtle contemporary acting . . . Davis's Mildred occasionally seems too mannered and overwrought. Her bravura performance undoubtedly grips the attention but in her tirades . . . [she] seems out of control and makes it difficult to understand why so cultured a gentleman would tolerate such a guttersnipe."

I recently saw the film twice and, in the first half, she now seems almost a caricature of her later self. At both performances the audience laughed at Davis throughout the early parts of the film. Yet in the later scenes I found her powerfully moving, relentless and startling. She was nominated for an Academy Award for this performance but lost to Claudette Colbert.

Her next film, *Housewife,* was with George Brent, Ann Dvorak and John Halliday. Davis wore attractive clothes and looked good but the picture was a letdown after *Bondage*. Frank S. Nugent in the New York *Times* commented on "the bewildering regularity with which the unexpected fails to happen" and found "Miss Davis a trifle too obvious as the siren."

For forty years Davis has been commenting bitterly, if not accurately, on not getting the much-coveted role of Scarlett O'Hara in *Gone With the Wind*. Disregarding easily verifiable facts, she continues to insist that Jack Warner "bought" the novel for her but that she turned it down without reading it when she went to England on strike. An interesting story—but true?

Before the book was ever published, David Selznick purchased *Gone With the Wind,* in July 1936. He was the sole owner of motion picture rights and no one else, including Jack Warner, ever had even an option on the property. Through the many years since GWTW was first released, Davis has declared, "It was insanity that I not be given Scarlett! It could have been written for me"; and, another time, "I was as perfect for Scarlett as Clark Gable was for Rhett Butler." She still blames George Cukor (originally the director for GWTW but replaced by Victor Fleming) for giving Vivien Leigh the role. "He still saw me as the girl in *Broadway* and, whatever his ancient grievance, his thumbs were still down." Selznick, who produced, cast and made *all* final decisions on *Gone With the Wind*, has written of casting Scarlett: "Why didn't I give up the idea of a new girl and get Bette Davis? Well, there were as many people against Bette Davis as there were for her—maybe more! Even had we wanted Miss Davis in preference to a new personality, Warner Bros. wouldn't give up Bette Davis for a picture to be released by M-G-M."

Selznick wanted a new face for Scarlett; he felt that a well-known actress would be nowhere near as effective. In spite of tremendous pressure to cast a Star in the role, he instigated the greatest talent search Hollywood had ever seen, and it was his decision, not Cukor's, to cast Vivien Leigh.

Surely Davis is well aware of all this. She was hardly alone in longing to play Scarlett; nearly every actress under fifty felt that she could—and should—play the role. Katharine Hepburn, who had been brought to Hollywood by Selznick and Cukor for *A Bill of Divorcement* and made several subsequent films with them, firmly declared, "The part was practically written for me. I *am* Scarlett O'Hara!" But even her close friendship with Selznick and Cukor was no help in securing the part. Jean Arthur, Miriam Hopkins, Joan Crawford, Norma Shearer, Margaret

Sullavan, Carole Lombard, Paulette Goddard and Tallulah Bankhead were among the leading contenders. Bankhead commented, "I was inflamed with the desire to play Scarlett. I felt I had the qualifications . . . the looks, the Southern background and breeding, the proper accent." When she was tested and deemed too old, she persisted, "I'll go to my grave convinced that I could have drawn the cheers of Longstreet, Beauregard and Robert E. Lee had I been permitted to wrestle with Clark Gable."

As all the world must know, the role of Scarlett was finally given to Vivien Leigh, who played it brilliantly and won an Academy Award in 1939. The very similar role of Julie in *Jezebel* was given to Bette Davis, who played it brilliantly and won her Academy Award in 1938.

Here is Davis (with Franchot Tone, top left) as she looked in *Dangerous*, in which she gave a bravura performance that *did* win her an Academy Award and holds up well today. Her career was gaining real impetus with such mature films as this and the soon to follow *Bordertown* and *The Petrified Forest*.

In 1937, Davis was teamed with Henry Fonda in *That Certain Woman* (top right), and again the following year in *Jezebel* (bottom left). The latter was the first of her three exceptionally fine films (*The Letter* and *The Little Foxes*) directed by William Wyler. *Jezebel* (bottom right), which added new dimensions to her already impressive acting range, won her a second Academy Award.

One of the most memorable scenes in *Jezebel* occurs when Julie (Davis) insists on wearing a scarlet dress to the 1950 Olympus Ball in New Orleans in-

stead of the customary white dress decreed by tradition. A similar incident had occurred in Hollywood a short time before *Jezebel* was filmed, and probably was the basis for its inclusion in the film plot: Carole Lombard, noted for her party-ideas, was asked to be hostess for the 1936 Mayfair Ball. She decided on an all-white motif, so the ladies were asked—and agreed —to dress in white, only white! All did, and the Ball was the snowy perfection envisioned until Norma Shearer made a late entrance wearing a spectacular scarlet gown. She caused the same consternation as did Davis in *Jezebel* and, naturally, endeared herself to the other ladies . . . Screenwriter John Huston was there and, no doubt, when he helped adapt the stage play, was responsible for putting this extraordinary happening into the movie.

Davis in *The Sisters,* a costume drama set at the turn of the century during the presidency of Theodore Roosevelt. Critic Graham Greene thought it "worth seeing for the sake of the adroit period production and the fragile, pop-eyed acting of Miss Bette Davis." Readers of the book, the critics and Davis herself deplored the film's happy ending, which the studio changed from the novel.

(A new scene had been added reuniting Errol Flynn and Davis; as William Dean Howells once told Edith Wharton, "What the American public always wants is a tragedy with a happy ending." Warner Bros. and many screen fans agreed.)

Davis made screen tests for the coveted role of the young novice in a proposed film version of the famed Max Reinhardt stage spectacle, *The Miracle.* It was to have been her first color film but the project was abandoned because of script problems.

Ronald Reagan and Davis in *Dark Victory*

Conrad Nagel (right) visits the set of *Dark Victory* in 1939. He had been the star of Davis' very first film, *Bad Sister,* at Universal studios in 1931. Humphrey Bogart had a supporting role in both films.

Unquestionably, 1939 was the peak of Davis' career. Released that year were four prestigious and highly successful films, *Dark Victory, Juarez, The Old Maid* and *The Private Lives of Elizabeth and Essex.* Warner Bros. began touting her as "First Lady of the Screen," a title they had conferred only a few years earlier on Ruth Chatterton, who was now considered passé. M-G-M applied the "First Lady" tag to Norma Shearer, while Katharine Hepburn was RKO's choice for that honor. On Broadway, Ethel Barrymore, Katharine Cornell, Helen Hayes and Lynn Fontanne contended for "First Lady of the Theater" but, with so many outstanding acting talents enriching both mediums and the rapid fluctuations of careers, it was well-nigh impossible for any star to claim that title for any length of time.

By the late 30's, when Davis reached her peak, Dietrich, Carole Lombard and Claudette Colbert were the top female stars at Paramount; Irene Dunne, Ginger Rogers and Katharine Hepburn vied for that position at RKO; and M-G-M had Garbo, Shearer and Crawford jockeying for the crown, followed closely by Myrna Loy, Jeanette MacDonald and (by 1940) Katharine Hepburn, as well.

But at Warner Bros., where she had no real feminine competition, there was no doubt in anyone's mind that Bette Davis was the queen of the lot!

With George Brent and Miriam Hopkins in *The Old Maid* (1939). In London, film critic Graham Greene wrote, "Her performance . . . is of extraordinary virtuosity—as the young girl, and the secret mother, and the harsh, prim middle-aged woman with her tiny lines and her talcum. It is like a manual of acting for beginners in three lessons" (*The Spectator*, January 19, 1940) (top left, opposite).

With Errol Flynn in *The Private Lives of Elizabeth and Essex,* also 1939. For the role of Elizabeth, Davis shaved her hairline back several inches and her eyebrows off, replacing them with high penciled ones. A pasty white makeup helped age the thirty-one-year-old actress into a remarkable semblance of the sixty-year-old monarch (top right, bottom left, opposite).

In 1936, Flora Robson had played Elizabeth in the British production, *Fire Over England,* with Laurence Olivier and Vivien Leigh. According to Robson's interpretation, Elizabeth was a hot-tempered but still level-headed Queen, while Davis portrayed her with definite neurotic and vacillating attitudes. She wanted Warner Bros. to borrow Olivier for the role of Essex and was not happy playing opposite Flynn.

He and Davis couldn't have been more dissimilar in attitude, temperament or background. Fun-loving and casual on the surface, Flynn was a man of tremendous good looks and charm, one to whom everything came easily. The theater-trained Davis had had to compete with the great beauties of Hollywood for stardom, and won that position by becoming tough, shrewd and dedicated to her art. It was inevitable that they wouldn't mesh. Flynn wrote of this filming, ". . . she was a far better actress than I could ever hope to be an actor . . . a dynamic creature, the big star of the lot . . . but not physically my type." Davis has commented often through the years of her dissatisfaction at playing opposite Flynn and remains patronizing about his talent and ability, an opinion not shared by some of Flynn's other contemporaries.

In 1955, Davis again played Elizabeth in the British film, *The Virgin Queen,* with a performance she and some critics thought superior to her original interpretation of that role (bottom right, opposite).

This 1939 portrait was taken just after she played Elizabeth, so she has false eyebrows and a front hairpiece (top).

As French governess Henriette Deluzy in *All This, and Heaven Too* (1940). Charles Boyer was co-starred in this film, a moving, meticulous drama based on a popular Rachel Field novel (center).

The Letter (1940) was one of her best films, a superior melodrama acted by a superb cast and directed with a firm hand by William Wyler. There is general agreement that this was one of Davis' most admirable performances, and it remains a highlight of her career (right).

As the Empress Carlotta in *Juarez,* Davis was gorgeous to behold in spectacular and authentic-looking clothes designed by Orry-Kelly. The ball gown was an exact replica of a dress worn by Carlotta.

In the early portions of the film, when the young Empress arrives in Mexico, Davis was dressed in appropriate light colors. But later, to characterize Carlotta's advancing madness, her clothes became darker and darker until finally, completely insane, she was garbed entirely in black.

Portraits from *The Little Foxes* (top left), *The Man Who Came to Dinner* (bottom) and *In This Our Life* (right).

Note the many "looks" that Davis brought to her characterizations: each role effected a change in the shape of her mouth and eyebrows, kind of hair style and mode of dressing. During the early phase of her career, when she compared herself to other stars, Davis felt that she was not a beauty. She envied the glamorous treatment received by stars at M-G-M (Garbo, Crawford, Harlow) and Paramount (Dietrich, Lombard, Colbert). By comparison, it's true that Warner Bros., primarily a man's studio, seemed to lag behind other studios in this respect. But after 1938 she *was* the queen of the Warner Bros. studio and had become such an outstanding star in Hollywood that she was able to demand the Superstar treatment with its every prerogative. One result was a much more natural look in her screen appearance, a distinct improvement on the studios' former attempts at glamour.

These photographs, all from *Now, Voyager,* show three phases in the life of Charlotte Vale: the young ingenue, the repressed spinster and the transformed woman. Few other stars have gone to such extensive detail in makeup or garbed themselves so unbecomingly as did Davis in this film.

With Dietrich and Bob Hope as Hollywood went to war in 1942

With Hal Wallis, her producer at Warner Bros., at an Academy Award dinner

With Norma Shearer (left) and Miriam Hopkins in 1938

With Charles Boyer and her mother, Ruth Favor Davis, at the première of *All This, and Heaven Too* in 1940

With Hedda Hopper at a 1950 radio broadcast

Davis attends a film showing after filming *Elizabeth and Essex* for which she shaved her eyebrows and forehead; bangs cover the short hair growing back to normal.

HUSBANDS

Davis said of her four marriages, "If I was a fool in my private life, I can't blame my profession for that."

Harmon Nelson (right), whom she married in August 1932, before she became the career-consumed Star. Her interest in Howard Hughes was thought to have caused the breakup of this marriage.

Arthur Farnsworth and Davis (below) were married December 31, 1940. He died of a fall on August 25, 1943.

Mr. and Mrs. William Grant Sherry with friends C. W. and Bridget Price at their November 1945 wedding reception (center right). The couple had one child, Barbara Davis Sherry, born May 1, 1947. Sherry and Davis divorced in 1949.

Gary Merrill. After their marriage on July 29, 1950, the couple adopted two children, Margo and Michael. Seen here with Carl Sandburg in 1959 (bottom right) when they toured from Maine to California in the stage production *The World of Carl Sandburg*. Following her divorce from Merrill in 1960, Davis swore off marriage.

In no other film, not even *Now, Voyager*, did Davis run such a gamut of looks and age as in *Mr. Skeffington* (1944). Her complete transformation from a young woman who was a great beauty into the incredibly ravaged old lady of the final scenes was a feat of remarkable skill. Her clothes, designed by Orry-Kelly, ranged from the hobble skirts of 1914 through the flapper age into the 30's and 40's, and the whole performance, a tour de force, remains one of her most praised, even though most critics considered the film itself a super soap opera.

A Stolen Life, '46

The next year, 1945, Davis portrayed an English schoolmistress who taught in a Welsh mining town in *The Corn Is Green.*

Deception, '46

James Cagney in *The Bride Came C.O.D.*, 1941

MALE CO-STARS

Among her illustrious male co-stars have been such names as Leslie Howard, Errol Flynn, Henry Fonda, George Brent, Franchot Tone (all pictured elsewhere), Paul Muni, Edward G. Robinson, Paul Lukas, Claude Rains, Joseph Cotten and Alec Guinness. Here are:

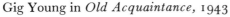

Gig Young in *Old Acquaintance*, 1943

Herbert Marshall in *The Letter*, 1940

Charles Boyer (with Barbara O'Neil and young Richard Nichols) in *All This, and Heaven Too,* 1940

Paul Henreid and John Loder in *Now, Voyager,* 1942

Robert Montgomery in *June Bride,* 1948

Brian Aherne in *Juarez,* 1939

Glenn Ford on the set of
A Stolen Life, 1946

FEMALE CO-STARS

Olivia de Havilland made four films with Davis: *It's Love I'm After, Elizabeth and Essex, In This Our Life* and *Hush . . . Hush, Sweet Charlotte,* and they have remained friends during their long careers.

Miriam Hopkins and Davis were not friends; each had a well-deserved reputation for temperament and the constant clash when they filmed *The Old Maid* and *Old Acquaintance* made film history.

Mary Astor also made two films with Davis, but *they* were mutual admirers. Astor won an Academy Award for her "supporting role" in *The Great Lie* in 1941, and appeared in 1964 with Davis and De Havilland in *Hush . . . Hush, Sweet Charlotte.* Mary Astor wrote of *The Great Lie,* "People have said that I 'stole' the picture from Bette Davis, but that is sheer nonsense. She handed it to me on a silver platter." When Astor won her Academy Award for Best Supporting Actress, Davis wired her from her home in Vermont, "We *did* it. Congratulations, baby."

The most spectacular teaming was that of Joan Crawford and Davis in *What Ever Happened to Baby Jane?* Although the film had an interesting story line, a decaying *Sunset Boulevard* setting and post-*Psycho* horrors, the combination of Davis and Crawford was the film's principal raison d'être. This unique commodity, a box office smash, was scheduled to be repeated in *Hush . . . Hush,* but Crawford became ill after a week of shooting and her long hospitalization caused producer Bob Aldrich to substitute Olivia de Havilland in that role.

Here she is in a pre-production rehearsal photo with Joseph Cotten and Crawford before Crawford was forced to relinquish her role.

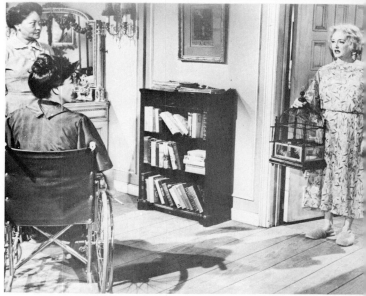

Susan Hayward, like Joan Crawford, Mary Astor and Olivia de Havilland, was an Academy Award winner (*I Want to Live,* 1958). She and Davis had a combined total of fifteen Academy Award nominations. Years before they appeared together in the 1964 *Where Love Has Gone, Time* magazine described Davis as "The Duse of the Depression Era" and Hayward as "A bargain-basement Davis."

SCREEN TESTS

As mentioned throughout this chapter, no one else was more conscientious about every detail of a role than Betty Davis. Here are examples—tests made in various makeups, wigs and costumes.

Hair and makeup tests for *The Great Lie*. Davis did not like the wig (above) so went home and cut her hair as seen below.

Two blonde wigs for *Fashions of 1934*

Tests (left) and end results (right) for *The Corn Is Green* (top) and *Mr. Skeffington* (bottom). Test shots from *Now, Voyager* (left) and *All This, and Heaven Too* (right) are at center.

Probably no other actress in history is more identified with a cigarette than Bette Davis. On and off the screen, it is a part of her—used to punctuate every sentence—every gesture—every thought and voice intonation. Rex Reed has described her as looking "as if she were walking in a cumulus cloud." Walter Kerr commented that often she "miraculously managed to snatch six or seven quick drags per sentence—often puffing up such a billowing aura about her that the enhanced production values were all but obscured."

The cigarette industry need never fear a decline as long as Bette Davis is about—to light still another cigarette plucked from the sterling silver case inscribed with John F. Kennedy's inaugural invitation given to her in 1960 by Frank Sinatra.

Davis' performance in *All About Eve* has been described by Richard Schickel as "an epochal summation of the Davis screen character"; for it, she received the New York Film Critics Circle Award for the best female performance of 1950, the San Francisco Critics' Award, and her eighth Academy Award nomination. It was an ironic coincidence that *Eve,* the best movie Hollywood ever made about the theater, was released the same year as *Sunset Boulevard,* the best movie ever made about the screen. Both films contended for an extraordinarily large number of Academy Award nominations in every field, and many people think that the choice for best actress between Gloria Swanson and Bette Davis was such an impossibly difficult one that Judy Holliday won by default over the more solid work of the two veteran actresses.

"If I had lost to Miss Swanson in *Sunset Boulevard,* which was marvelous, I would have done so with great, great graciousness," commented Davis. I couldn't agree more with her in her opinion of actors and actresses who play a role on the stage for a long period before transferring it to film: "It's not that big an accomplishment—not as challenging as starting from scratch to play the character on the screen." Too often, Academy Awards have been given to warmed-over stage performances by people whose contributions to the screen will never, ever match those of Bette Davis or Gloria Swanson.

All About Eve was an unqualified triumph for Davis and for everyone connected with it, winning unanimous praise from audiences and critics.

Dorothy Manners: "It is the sharpest, truest, most sophisticated and titillating performance of the season." Alton Cook, New York *World-Telegram:* "Bette Davis, for nearly two decades one of our greatest actresses and worst performers, finally is shaken out of her tear-jerking formula and demonstrates what a vivid, over-whelming force she possesses." Leo Mishkin, New York *Morning Telegraph:* "Bette Davis gives the finest, most compelling and most perceptive performance she has ever played on the screen."

Facing Anne Baxter (who later played Margo Channing, the Davis role, on the stage in *Applause*) with Gary Merrill, Celeste Holm, George Sanders, Marilyn Monroe and Hugh Marlowe in the background.

HAIR STYLES

As these photographs illustrate, Davis has worn her hair in every conceivable style and color. The hue has ranged from her original light brown through platinum blonde to jet black. The character of the role she played determined the type of face makeup, the mode of dress and the color and style of her hair. (A secretary would have a subdued coiffure; a frivolous person, something more ornate.) Since her ears didn't match (the left one protruded more and had a rounder shape), her hair was seldom worn up or away from the face. If so, a small curl was usually brushed over the ears to disguise this difference in appearance.

As it must to all performers, there came a period of decline in Davis' career. At forty-four, unable to find suitable scripts that would match the work she had so proudly done, Davis began what she would later describe as her "ten black years." Not only had she matured, but Hollywood had changed. She was no longer under contract to a major studio with the many advantages such an organization could offer her. And there were "new faces," though certainly not better ones.

Both she, and the films she chose to make, came in for severe comment. The Hollywood *Reporter* wrote that she gave "a performance that you'd expect to find from a night club impersonation of the actress." *Films in Review* commented on "the asperity which recently has increasingly infected her performances." And London critic Richard Winninger summed it up this way: "Miss Davis, with more say than most stars as to what films she makes, seems to have lapsed into egoism. The criterion for her choice of film would appear to be that nothing must compete with the full display of each facet of the Davis art. Only bad films are good enough for her."

In reviewing the Davis career, I am struck by the lengthy list of distinguished pictures she made in a very short period which were adaptations of Broadway plays. From 1938 to 1945, she starred in twelve such productions: *Jezebel, Dark Victory, The Old Maid, The Private Lives of Elizabeth and Essex, The Letter, The Little Foxes, The Man Who Came to Dinner, Watch on the Rhine, Old Acquaintance* and *The Corn Is Green*. In so doing, she became the screen counterpart of the most prestigious ladies of the theater: Lynn Fontanne, Ethel Barrymore, Tallulah Bankhead, Katharine Cornell, Jane Cowl and Helen Menken.

None of Davis' contemporaneous rivals, not even her nearest competitor, Norma Shearer (the "First Lady" of M-G-M), could match this list in quantity or quality. Shearer was the wife of Irving Thalberg, head of production at that studio and a man directly responsible for the careers of a number of top people on the Metro lot. But no one else (Crawford, Garbo, Loy, Marion Davies) was assigned such prestigious stage hits as Shearer, who filmed *The Trial of Mary Dugan, Let Us Be Gay, Private Lives, Strange Interlude, Idiot's Delight* and *The Barretts of Wimpole Street*. (Marion Davies left M-G-M to go to Warner Bros. because Thalberg took *The Barretts* away from her and gave it to Shearer.) Garbo got *Anna Christie* and *Romance,* and Crawford received her one Broadway hit, *Susan and God,* only after Shearer turned it down.

In addition to these Broadway shows, Davis also filmed some highly successful novels of the day: *The Sisters; All This, and Heaven Too; Now, Voyager; The Great Lie; In This Our Life* and *Mr. Skeffington* (which she refers to as *Mrs. Skeffington* in her autobi-

ography). During this same period, it is true, she played in a few other films that were not of the same caliber. But, in the long history of entertainment, no star—male or female—has been able to maintain only first-rate successes. Davis fought harder than most for quality—and usually won.

The Star, 1952

Payment on Demand (one of my favorite Davis films) and *Another Man's Poison* (apparently *no one's* favorite) followed *All About Eve.* Good parts were getting harder to find. Then Davis was offered *The Star,* a picture about a top film actress and Academy Award winner who had become a destitute "has-been." Davis was splendid with her candid, acute portrayal of the demise of a Hollywood "Star" and her rebirth as a "person."

An interesting comparison is the early (1931) portrait taken when she was a film novice at Universal.

A portrait at the time of *The Catered Affair* (above, 1956), in which she played the Bronx wife of Ernest Borgnine and mother of Debbie Reynolds.

In 1962 her autobiography, *The Lonely Life,* was published and this portrait was used for the back of the book jacket.

PAINTINGS

When Davis graduated from Cushing at seventeen, her mother made this readily recognizable silhouette of her.

A 1933 charcoal sketch by Charles Sheldon, who photographed Davis for a series of magazine covers. His photograph is an interesting contrast to the studio portraits of that time.

Davis stands in front of the painting of herself as the young, beautiful Fanny Skeffington for the 1944 film *Mr. Skeffington* (left).

With her portrait from *Jezebel*

FASHION

Bette Davis might not be the first name to come to mind in connection with screen fashion; her personality was so strong that often it tended to overwhelm whatever she wore. Also, clothes were important to her only to the degree in which they helped portray the character of a role. Unless a part called for it, she had little thought for fashion and glamour.

It is a surprise to find how much, indeed, she was involved in fashion during her younger days, and the frequency with which she posed for such layouts. In the beginning there was the Constance Bennett look: softly sculptured hair, society-woman clothes and model stance. By the time of *Fashions of 1934,* she was dressed in a very slick Hollywood style, almost M-G-M-like in its extremes, and a contrast to her later look.

As she matured as an actress and Star, she began to take on a new look for each part, and her clothes give us a perfect catalogue of 30's and 40's fashion. Although it was probably not her intention to do so, she created styles and made fashion news: the strapless red dress from *Jezebel* and the caps from *Dark Victory* are just two examples that went from the screen into the wardrobes of her fashion-conscious fans.

She wore clothes with ease and authority despite a less than perfect figure, large breasts and a neck that was too long and broad. Orry-Kelly did the bulk of her screen clothes from 1933 to 1946 and years later, in 1959, designed two evening gowns for her to wear on stage in *The World of Carl Sandburg*. She always speaks highly of him and says that he, like Edith Head, knew how to dress ladies as well as glamour queens. Both designers understood that their creations were not meant to be the star of a production or film but to enhance the actress wearing them.

For many years Edith Head designed clothes for Davis and collaborated with her "unflagging perfectionism and professional occupation" as it applied to the characterization of her roles. Davis is lavish in her praise of Head, describing her work as "brilliant. . . . She designed some of the most beautiful modern clothes I had ever worn. . . . I was fortunate to have my wardrobe in her genius, capable hands."

Among the Davis films for which Edith Head did the clothes are *June Bride, All About Eve, Beyond the Forest, Payment on Demand, Pocketful of Miracles, Where Love Has Gone* and *Madame Sin*.

Davis claims that Hal Wallis, head of production at Warner Bros., took an inordinate interest in hats and imposed his own taste in them on Orry-Kelly's designs, so she subscribed to *Vogue* magazine in his name with the hope that he would become familiar with contemporary hat trends and styles. "Orry-Kelly designed the outfits but Mr. Wallis designed the hats —and always the same one!"

RECENT YEARS

As Catherine the Great in *John Paul Jones,* 1959, with Robert Stack

At the time of *The Anniversary,* 1968

The Scapegoat, 1959

Hush . . . Hush, Sweet Charlotte, 1964

Madame Sin, 1972. Edith Head did the wardrobe —black gowns to match the black palace and black Rolls-Royce. A black wig, a copy of one worn thirty-three years earlier in *Juarez,* false eyelashes and silver-blue mascara turned Davis' eyes into almonds for the required Eurasian look.

The past few years, when not filming, Davis has spent part of her time traveling with her one-woman show based on her segment of John Springer's "Legendary Ladies" series. Tammy Grimes, John Springer and Davis (in a Norell dress of white satin and black velvet) at an after-performance party the evening of her Town Hall appearance. Writer Ronald Bowers succinctly described the "loud, inarticulate audience largely populated with Judy Garland's old camp followers" who competed with film historians during the after-film question-and-answer period. Davis has taken this talk show to colleges across America and abroad to England, Wales, Scotland and Ireland.

RÉSUMÉ

At the 1977 American Film Institute's tribute to Bette Davis, amid the enthusiastic and understandable hyperbole of such an evening were the following comments:

Jane Fonda: "She redefined the words 'actress' and 'star.'"

George Stevens, Jr.: "She tested her range, playing mothers, molls, murderesses, a queen, a dowager, shrews and an actress."

Olivia de Havilland spoke of her as "an electric presence . . . an actress of courage who advanced movie making to an art. She broke new ground because she wanted to play real people, good and bad, whereas most actresses wanted to be only beautiful and good."

Director Joseph Mankiewicz said of Davis making *All About Eve,* "She was so co-operative I thought I was working with an impostor."

Hepburn and Davis are considered by many to be Hollywood's premier dramatic actresses and best technicians. Davis has been nominated ten times as Best Actress and has won twice. Only Hepburn has topped that impressive figure: she is the first player of either sex to have had eleven nominations and to win three starring awards.

Four times they have competed for the same award. First, in 1935 Hepburn's *Alice Adams* lost to Davis' *Dangerous.* Neither won the next two times: 1940 saw Hepburn nominated for *The Philadelphia Story* and Davis for *The Letter;* and in 1942, Davis was nominated for *Now, Voyager* and Hepburn for *Woman of the Year.* In 1962, Hepburn's performance in *Guess Who's Coming to Dinner?* won over Davis' *What ever Happened to Baby Jane?*

It is interesting to compare and contrast the style and personality of the two stars both on and off screen. As fashions in women have changed, both seem very contemporary in most of their old films. But whereas Hepburn, with her fiery independence, wanted only to prove she was the equal of the men in her films, Davis often seemed to be trying to prove that she was superior to them.

During the years, they both played opposite a number of the same leading men including Douglas Fairbanks, Jr., Franchot Tone, Charles Boyer, Spencer Tracy, Herbert Marshall, Paul Lukas, Brian Aherne, Paul Henreid and Humphrey Bogart.

The late Joan Crawford, when asked what stars she most admired, picked Hepburn and Davis to head her list because "they are so vastly talented and strong-willed and indestructible." Explaining that today it's a "totally different industry than the one I belonged to, so I'm not talking about many real stars in the old sense of the word," and comparing today's "stars" with the stars of her day she said, "We seemed to burn much brighter." Hepburn herself said, "There aren't many real stars now, in movies or in the theater: there are lots of talented people but few whom I would call real, real stars."

KATHARINE HEPBURN

In 1932, Katharine Hepburn burst upon the screens of the world with hurricane velocity, storming the senses and riveting the eye. It was a stunning debut, and so instantaneous was her triumph that RKO found itself taken by surprise. For many years, Hollywood had been accustomed to building stars slowly and surely, planning each step in a long-range campaign. Consequently, when after just one picture her studio discovered it had a new star on its hands, it was quite unprepared for her runaway success.

Indeed, up until this time in the entire history of motion pictures, I can recall only one other corresponding triumph. Just a year or so before, Marlene Dietrich had hit the screen with a similar explosion when Paramount introduced the German import to American audiences in *Morocco* and then, for additional impact, released the previously filmed *The Blue Angel*. Literally, Dietrich became an International Star overnight, setting a precedent difficult for others to try to follow. Similar attempts were made for foreign actresses Anna Sten, Gwili Andre, Lil Dagover, Tala Birell and Isa Miranda, but none succeeded.

It's interesting to recall that during their first year in Hollywood both Dietrich and Hepburn were compared and contrasted with Greta Garbo, then the criterion by which actresses were judged. An intensity similar to Joan Crawford's was noted in Hepburn's work, and the comparison to two of the screen's Top Goddesses was, of course, excellent publicity for the newcomer. It soon was evident, however, that neither Dietrich nor Hepburn was a copy of anyone but instead were unique personalities who had created new patterns for stardom.

In retrospect, Garbo also has been described as "an overnight star," but the fact is that it took over two years for her name to be billed above a picture title and then as co-star with John Gilbert. Her solo stardom took three years, for Hollywood *did* build slowly then. It took Joan Crawford five, Bette Davis six, and Myrna Loy nine years to become stars, so the cases of Hepburn and Dietrich were unique.

Then lightning struck the screen a third time with Mae West. Introduced in George Raft's *Night After Night* (in which, in Raft's words, "she walked off with the picture"), Paramount immediately starred her in *She Done Him Wrong*. She, too, became a world-wide sensation and a third legend had arrived. These three women—Hepburn, Dietrich and West— broke the accepted mold for star-building in a very short period, a feat that has never been duplicated since on quite the same scale. Remarkable then, it is even more remarkable some forty years later that all three have remained potent theatrical powers.

Hepburn came to the screen from the Broadway stage, as did West, Bette Davis, Henry Fonda, Clark Gable, Claudette Colbert, Irene Dunne and Spencer Tracy. Holdovers from silent pictures included such outstanding stars as Ronald Colman, Gary Cooper, William Powell, Garbo, Crawford, Loy, Del Rio, Norma Shearer and Carole Lombard. All of them belonged to that generation of actors and actresses who, by their mere presence on the screen, attracted us every week to the movie theaters and aroused our interest in whatever parts they played. We admired them, fantasized about them, and wanted to be like them. In spite of some forgettable pictures and mediocre roles, there was total involvement whenever they appeared.

Some of today's crop are probably better actors, although this is a moot point. But few are such vivid personalities. In the past two years a shark and an ape —both mechanical!—have been among the most widely seen and discussed screen characters. Today's fame and popularity are certainly inclined to be ephemeral so that one can't help but wonder which of the present "stars" will be of interest in future decades.

What is it that makes a Star? Ever since the beginning of theater this question has been asked and answered in various ways, from differing points of view.

George Cukor, who has directed probably more Superstars than anyone else in Hollywood (Garbo, Cary Grant, Crawford, Harlow, Tracy, Barrymore, Beery, W. C. Fields, Colbert, Garland, March, et al.), has said, "The Star system is the cult of personality. And while it may be personality, rather than talent, that catches the eye and attention in the first place, if the talent doesn't develop, it grows threadbare."

Katharine Hepburn, who ranks high among that high-wattage nucleus of legendary women Superstars (Swanson, Davis, Garbo, Crawford, West, Dietrich) has commented, "I think all good actors are personalities. If they're not, they're not stars. Just go through the list: Chaplin, Mary Pickford, Douglas Fairbanks, William S. Hart, Tom Mix, Lillian Gish. And then get into Joan Crawford, Bette Davis, Norma Shearer, Greta Garbo. They all had strong, strong personalities. What makes you a star is horsepower.

"The only idol I had as a kid was the cowboy star, William S. Hart. I was mad for him. But I don't think I was ever really a hero-worshiper. Blind hero-worship for a fellow egomaniac is impossible. That's why I understand the cold eye of youth . . . I once gave it to Jack Barrymore.

"My two favorite actors have been Spencer Tracy and Laurette Taylor—both Irish, both as fundamental as a baked potato.

"Great performing is total simplification—the capacity to get to the essence of it—to eliminate all the frills and foibles. You rely on absolute concentration and truth. It's as simple as saying 'Thank you.'"

Hepburn's first film was a property that had made a star on the stage of another Katharine (Cornell) a decade earlier. It was a good role and a fine opportunity of which Hepburn herself said years later, "If you are new, if you haven't been seen before, you practically always steal the movie . . . lots of girls' parts are written that way."

Although *A Bill of Divorcement* remains of interest today primarily because it was Hepburn's film debut, it also had surprisingly touching performances by Barrymore and Billie Burke. Both are convincing and appealing. Hepburn's oddly attractive face and harsh, staccato voice required a little getting used to but her personality is so compelling that it's hard to take your eyes off her whenever she's on screen. She had star quality even then. Today that sandpaper voice, Bryn Mawr diction, arrogant but elegant manner, and distinctive face lacquered by mature distinction are readily recognizable the world over. She always had that country-fresh quality and the ambivalence of the gruff, straight-from-the-shoulder tomboy mixed with femininity—the female meeting the male on his own ground.

Hepburn had a brief, generally forgotten marriage to a Philadelphian named Ludlow Ogden Smith. They were married December 12, 1928, in the Hepburn home in West Hartford, Connecticut, during the period when she was beginning her stage career. Not wanting to be called "Kate Smith" or, indeed, just plain "Mrs. Smith," she persuaded her husband to legally change his name by dropping the surname and reversing the other two. Her role as Mrs. Ogden Ludlow was short-lived, however, for she soon resumed her theatrical career. Her husband seems to have been a shadowy figure who usually acceded to his headstrong wife's wishes; whether it was because he was so genuinely in love with her, or because it was easier to cope with any situation if it were just done Kate's way, is not known.

The couple was separated in 1932 by Kate's film career but they remained friendly. Then, in 1934, after *The Lake* closed, she sailed on March 18 for Europe. When she returned April 4, she left immediately for Mérida, Yucatán, where she petitioned for a divorce. It was granted on May 9. Because of uncertainty about the validity of the Mexican divorce, Ludlow sued Hepburn for divorce in 1942. When it was granted, he remarried in five days and thereafter remained out of Hepburn's limelight.

Hepburn never remarried and has always refused to discuss this. *But* she has said, "I don't believe in marriage because it's not a natural institution! Otherwise, why sign a contract for it?"

When Katharine Hepburn made her movie debut in *A Bill of Divorcement,* she had an electrifying impact on the public although her appearance and personality hadn't yet come to terms with the technical aspects of the camera. With that total concentration for which she was to become famed, she studied her camera self and the technique of film, learning her screen potential so thoroughly that the following year she won her first Academy Award for her performance in *Morning Glory.*

Now, after nearly fifty years of being first a personality, then an actress, and eventually a Superstar, Katharine Hepburn has become a catalogue of memorable moments in the movies. Many of these moments occurred in her films of the 30's (*Little Women, Alice Adams, Holiday*), the 40's (*The Philadelphia Story, Woman of the Year, Adam's Rib*) and the 50's (*The African Queen, Summertime, The Rainmaker*). Continued revivals of these films, TV showings and film festivals have enabled new audiences to discover and savor her special qualities, so that today Hepburn is considered "a sort of national treasure." Her directness and ability to infuse a film with sincerity and warmth make her seem very contemporary, even when the film itself appears dated.

In her early films Hepburn often played an aggressive woman, one determined to hold her own in a man's world. In her middle period (*Summertime, The Rainmaker, The African Queen*), she was the wistful, lonely spinster, eager for a man. Finally she became the strong, sometimes imperious mother and matron; quick and precise but still loving and tender. It's been quite a range of roles!

Famed through the years as a great personality, an enduring actress and a really thorny dame, she remains a fiercely independent individual who somehow is still an endearing one, capable of great tenderness, unlimited generosity and sensitive vulnerability. As an actress, she has stripped away most of the cloying mannerisms that marred earlier performances so that her warm honesty, odd aristocratic manner and elegant beauty still captivate the eye and intrigue the mind.

Born in 1907–8–9 (take your choice), Kate was one of six children. Tom, her oldest brother (shown here), died at age sixteen. There still are her two sisters, Marion and Peg, and two brothers, Bob and

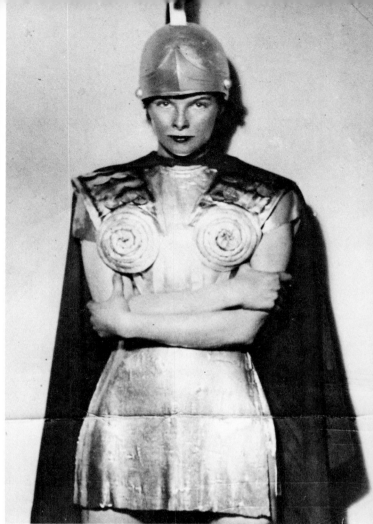

Dick. "I was wildly ambitious as a child, encouraged by my mother and father. We had a sense of family.

"Recently someone asked me, 'Kate, do you still see your family?' 'Of course,' I said. 'They're mine.'"

In 1928 she went to New York to try for the stage. Her father didn't approve of the theater but sent her twenty-five dollars with the excuse, "I won this gambling on the golf course. I don't approve of gambling and I don't approve of what you're doing. So I think this money ought to be yours."

Hepburn as she appeared in the Broadway production of *The Warrior's Husband* in 1932. Her eighth Broadway appearance and first unqualified hit, it led to a Hollywood contract (above right).

Right from the beginning, Hollywood began to turn Hepburn into a glamour girl. RKO, who had Irene Dunne, Ginger Rogers, Ann Harding and Fay Wray under contract, wanted its own Garbo, Dietrich or Crawford, and Hepburn proved just right to fill that need.

In her first few films, like all newcomers, she was given the standard Hollywood makeup treatment: i.e., copying bits and pieces from contemporary beauties. Superimposed on her were the Garbo eye makeup and hair style, the Dietrich butterfly-wing eyebrows and hollowed cheeks (from *Shanghai Express*), and Crawford's melon mouth and wide-shouldered look as worn that year in *Letty Lynton* (see next page).

Hepburn retained what was most becoming to her and, by her third or fourth film, became her own sort of beauty with a unique look—an oddly fascinating face with an angular body. Through the years, she evolved and matured into that phenomenon the world knows as "Kate," one of the great ornaments of the screen.

Immediately after filming *A Bill of Divorcement,* and before anyone realized that RKO had a potentially Big Star under contract, Hepburn left Hollywood for a European vacation without making arrangements with the studio for contact while abroad. When the picture was released and Hepburn's impact on the public was evident, RKO realized that it knew almost as little about its new hope as did the curious public. Since she was unavailable for consultation, the studio's publicity department was forced to cope as best it could with the multitude of eager inquiries about its recently discovered attraction. The result was a series of conflicting stories: she was a wealthy debutante; she was a poor girl from an average family; she was married; she was single; she had children; she did not. The turmoil and confusion were soon aided and abetted by the lady herself.

Hepburn alone and with John Barrymore in *A Bill of Divorcement*

When Hepburn returned to America on the *Paris,* she was met at the dock by a battery of inquiring reporters eager to learn something of the new mystery star. Shy, reserved and inexperienced in such matters, she took refuge in tongue-in-cheek answers, evading personal questions about herself and her family, and denying whatever facts the reporters had been able to dig up on her background and experience. "They asked, I thought, idiotic questions—so I gave them idiotic answers. I made up some ludicrous replies . . . and they printed everything! I thought they'd be smart enough to see through [my answers] but they weren't. I felt then that the press was my natural enemy," an attitude that Hepburn maintained for many years.

Subsequently, it was to take quite a while before the true facts of Hepburn's past and background were sorted out. She was always a very private person who took exceptional care to guard her personal life and she has remained so to this day.

For her second film, RKO went all out in promoting its new sensation. Billing her as "The Girl Who Set the World Aflame!" they proclaimed her "More Thrilling . . . More Disturbing . . . More Fascinating Than Ever." By the time of *The Little Minister,* they modestly declaimed, "Only the greatest actress of her time could have breathed life into the most magnetic heroine of all time!" There is no record that she approved the effusive gushings, but none that she protested them, either.

However, if her studio, the public and some critics overpraised her, there *were* those who quickly became disenchanted. Like Bette Davis, Hepburn was to endure some rather severe pannings during her long career.

In her second film, *Christopher Strong,* Hepburn was starred as a career-minded aviatrix and her appearance in uniform reminded critics and the public of the then contemporary Amelia Earhart. Norbert Lusk wrote, "Katharine Hepburn rises superior to an indifferent picture and proves herself every inch a star. Magnetic, arresting, original, she still is the most striking discovery of last year and this."

The film gave further evidence of her contradictory personality—the aloof and haughty young woman who underneath was shy and a good sport. If *Christopher Strong* was not an unqualified success, its star was.

Like almost everyone else at the time, Hepburn was an admirer of Garbo, and some of her early portraits give evidence of this (see next spread).

Later she was to say, "I wouldn't put myself in the class of Garbo . . . as a legend, she's in a class by herself. Garbo is total mystery, the way actors should be. She has always been a mysterious sailboat who disappeared over the horizon the moment she felt she couldn't cope."

Strange, exotic
Katherine.

Katharine Hepburn and Colin Clive in the ecstasy of "The Great Desire."

KATHARINE HEPBURN

THE extraordinary rise of Katharine Hepburn revives faith in democracy, the screen and stout-hearted girls. Whether "The Great Desire" is a grand passion or a timid yearning will make no difference to the career of this dauntless, frank 1933 modern.

Ernest A. Bachrach

Next, Hepburn entered into a phase of striking, "crazy-looking" portraits in which she was lighted to emphasize her angular, bony look. It was claimed that she even put lipstick in her nostrils to accent them. Her unique, metallic voice coupled with this bony look made her a special favorite of impressionists and cartoonists. *The New Yorker* ran a cartoon of a young horse and an old horse in a field: the young horse is tossing her head while the old one remarks, "Someone told her she looks like Katharine Hepburn!" Recently she said, "It's becoming stylish now to look upon me as though I had always been lovely. We all say that I have a classic beauty with a delicately proportioned face.

"But, at the beginning, I was always caricatured as a horse!" These photographs show why.

During this period (1933, when she filmed *Morning Glory, Little Women* and *Spitfire*) Hepburn's off-screen behavior reflected the eccentric look of her photographs.

After she returned to Hollywood for her second film, she seemed determined to keep the movie industry in its place and to prove that she could rewrite the rules of conduct for a star to her own specifications. She entered upon a period of being an "off-screen madcap," during which she was rebellious, indifferent to advice, unpleasant and unco-operative. Even in an industry full of egomaniacs, Hepburn stood out; she fought senselessly with practically everyone from the top producer to the lowest technician. To the press she deliberately distorted the facts of her life and alternated being abusive and insulting with being candidly appealing and "the good sport." Her friend, director George Cukor, described her behavior as "sub-collegiate idiotic" and, of course, it created a very adverse environment for her co-workers and studio officials.

By the end of 1933 many people in and out of films were reacting quite negatively to Hepburn's capers and publicity antics. *Screenland* editor Delight Evans, who previously had been a big Hepburn booster, devoted her December 1933 Editor's Page to an open letter that began: "Dear Katharine Hepburn: Don't you dare cheapen the star of *Morning Glory* by any more silly kid stuff like the news pictures we've all been subjected to lately." Continuing in the same vein, she enumerated and deplored Hepburn's antics and outrageous behavior. Kate's fellow townsman, M. Oakley Christomer, wrote a letter to *Picture Play*, May 1934, which pleaded "Oh, Hepburn, behave!"

In the March 1934 *Photoplay*, that then esteemed film monthly, writer Kirtley Baskette took her to task in an article that said in part, "Off the screen, Katharine Hepburn has apparently attempted to construct a legend of mystery, à la Garbo. Instead of effectiveness, it has resulted in downright craziness. The madcap from Bryn Mawr's pranks resemble those of a schoolgirl putting on an act.

"On her arrival in Hollywood, she begged for seclusion and privacy, but her outfits were enough to stop the proverbial clock. Wanting to slip 'unnoticed' around Hollywood, she rented a spectacular foreign-made car to do it in, riding with her feet cocked up on the back of the front seat. She asked to be 'left alone —so alone' but insisted on standing in the middle of RKO Studio's streets or sitting in a busy studio doorway to read her mail.

"She went around the studio lot carrying a white monkey which she tied to the desks of the people she wanted to plague. She gambled with the publicity department whether she would grant an interview or not; shooed photographers away one minute then took it 'big' with a wide grin for them the next.

"She took an almost pathological delight in allowing the wildest tales to be broadcast about her, without denial. She was married, not married, the mother of six, definitely not one of the rich, social Hepburns from Hartford. She never went to Bryn Mawr."

Also in 1933, a fellow player in summer stock at Ivoryton, Connecticut, remarked, "Whatever her reasons for giving out those cockeyed yarns, be sure it's a good one. Kate is very canny and farsighted. She's not impulsive! In fact, everything she does is calculated and well thought out. . . . She was always certain that she was a fine actress and spoke of it occasionally as a statement of fact. She has amazing self-confidence."

Exasperated victims of Hepburn's abusive behavior and inverted snobbery got their revenge. She was made to appear so foolish and unappealing in print and photographs that, of course, the public was influenced by all the reaction. Her films were not as well received, and after the flop of *Spitfire* and the debacle of her stage play, *The Lake,* she returned to Hollywood, this time chastened and subdued. For once in her life, she seemed willing to co-operate and the result was much better press and studio relations.

Apropos of this stage of her development, I was interested in a recent Hepburn comment: "It's kind of the style to be a nut now and I've always liked nuts. I was a nut in my day." If she "grew up" in Hollywood, it's equally true that Hollywood grew up to her. Many of her early habits—wearing pants, driving a station wagon herself instead of being chauffeur-driven, living quietly—would cause no comment today. They would properly be considered very normal.

Very, very early in her Hollywood career, after only a few films, writer Jack Harrower interviewed some of Hepburn's male co-stars for an article in the October 1934 *New Movie* magazine. Their comments were universally complimentary and if Mr. Harrower received any adverse observations, they weren't used: John Barrymore, *A Bill of Divorcement:* "She is highly intelligent; the girl thinks clearly and to the point." Adolphe Menjou, *Morning Glory:* "To me, Katharine Hepburn is one of the greatest artists of the screen. She not only plays a part, she lives it." Douglas Fairbanks, Jr., also in *Morning Glory,* reputedly had been astonished and somewhat turned off by Hepburn's imperious and dictatorial behavior. He discreetly commented, "Working with Miss Hepburn was a most stimulating experience. She threw herself into her role with the intensity of a Bernhardt." And Ralph Bellamy said, "I went into *Spitfire* determined not to like her as a result of the stories I'd heard about her. But she disarmed me completely and won me over in short order. The thing I liked best about her was her honesty and sincerity." Paul Lukas, *Little Women:* "She made those who worked with her want to work harder because of her fire and enthusiasm. She has a definite commanding personality . . . a terrific determination to succeed." And Douglas Montgomery, also in *Little Women,* said, "I knew Katharine Hepburn in New York before she was a success and I think she is the most exciting girl I've ever known. She is wonderful to work with."

Many years later, after *The African Queen,* Humphrey Bogart was to say, "I don't think she tries to be a character—she is one!"

Hepburn in *Morning Glory,* for which she won her first Academy Award, with Douglas Fairbanks, Jr., and Adolphe Menjou.

As two old-fashioned heroines: Jo in *Little Women*, one of the biggest film hits of 1933, and Bobbie in *The Little Minister* (1934), which was a disappointment. Pandro S. Berman (who produced eight of Hepburn's fourteen films at RKO) commented, "By this time, I realized that Kate was not a Movie Star . . . in the sense that Crawford or Shearer were —actresses able to drag an audience into theaters by their own efforts. She was a hit only in hit pictures. She couldn't save a flop."

Three portraits that show the rapid metamorphosis of Hepburn's screen face.

1933   1935   1936

In *Sylvia Scarlett,* for plot purposes, Hepburn masqueraded as a boy for the first half of the film. *Time* commented, *"Sylvia Scarlett* reveals the interesting fact that Katharine Hepburn is better-looking as a boy than as a woman."

With Brian Aherne (below) in later sequences, after she had returned to femininity. It's regrettable that Hepburn didn't play *Peter Pan* in the 30's when she had the needed youth and boyishness.

"The Most Modern of Girls," as RKO dubbed her, made a surprising number of costume pictures: *Little Women, The Little Minister, Mary of Scotland, A Woman Rebels* and *Quality Street.* These early screen roles displayed a softer, more fragile side of the multifaceted Hepburn, a distinct contrast to her appearance and deportment in her more modern roles. She returned to costume roles in 1947 in *The Sea of Grass* and in her two Academy Award roles of the 60's in *Guess Who's Coming to Dinner?* and *The Lion in Winter. The Madwoman of Chaillot* also starred her in a costume role.

Mary of Scotland, 1936, with Fredric March

A Woman Rebels, 1936

Quality Street, 1937, with Franchot Tone

In an article entitled "13 Irresistible Women" for the August 1934 *Photoplay,* the superlatively skillful photographer, Baron George Hoyningen-Huene, picked Hepburn and Garbo as "faces supreme . . . beyond classification." Among his other "irresistible" faces were Lombard, Del Rio, Swanson, Dietrich and Loretta Young (his Hepburn portrait above).

Of *Quality Street,* Frank Nugent wrote in the New York *Times,* "Her Phoebe Throssel needs a neurologist more than a husband. Such flutterings and jitterings and twitchings, such hand-wringing and mouth quaverings, such runnings about and eyebrow raisings have not been seen on the screen in many a moon."

Calling Hepburn "Hollywood's most vital personality," he continued, "There is a fanatical expression in her eye and a dynamo inside her which make her slightest word or gesture take on enormous importance. With her flaring nostrils and harsh mouth, she could never be called beautiful, but her face has a dynamic quality which is more important to an actress than beauty. She is almost hypnotic. She is always young with a genuine Peter Pan quality about her. I should describe Katharine Hepburn as 'civilized'!"

Hepburn as she looked in *Stage Door.* The film production was altered so drastically from the stage play (by Edna Ferber and George S. Kaufman) that Kaufman scornfully inquired, "Why didn't they call it *Screen Door?*" (right top and bottom)

Despite Kaufman's objections, the picture *was* a hit —something Hepburn needed badly after the cool reception to her last four films. It and her next two pictures, *Bringing Up Baby* and *Holiday,* helped somewhat to restore her lagging prestige, but not enough. When she offered to buy back her contract from RKO, the studio accepted with alacrity.

To top it all, she (along with Garbo, Crawford, Astaire, Mae West, Dietrich and a few others) was declared "Box Office Poison" by the Independent Theater Owners of America, a group whose crystal ball for evaluating talent was obviously very clouded.

STAGE

Throughout her career, Hepburn has alternated between theater and screen: some critics thought the latter a more suitable medium for her. Acknowledging her vivid personality, one observed, "Miss Hepburn is not versatile, but she is unique."

After her initial screen success, she returned to the stage in 1933 in the disastrous *The Lake,* which is chiefly remembered for Dorothy Parker's bilious review and the comment, "Katharine Hepburn ran the gamut of emotions from A to B." During the short run of the play, Hepburn had sheets hung in the theater wings so she wouldn't be distracted by backstage activities. George S. Kaufman acidly commented, "She's afraid she might catch acting!"

Famed theater critic George Jean Nathan, in his March 1934 *Vanity Fair* review, wrote, "Katharine Hepburn scores a big artistic failure in a feeble English play . . . the current striking advantages in not being an actress are clearly perceptible in the case of the much discussed Miss Hepburn . . . who, it is quickly to be observed, has many of the qualities that may one day make her an artist of quality and position. She has the looks, the fine body, the sharp intelligence. . . . But that day, despite the fact that the motion picture audience already hysterically regards her as such an actress, is—for the theatre and drama —still far from being at hand."

Hepburn in Charlotte Brontë's *Jane Eyre,* which opened December 1936 in New Haven. It was decided to take the play on tour before bringing it to New York, but the reception was lukewarm. Rather than risk further criticism, Hepburn closed it. After *The Lake,* her next Broadway appearance *had* to be a hit.

It was!

Hepburn's triumphal return to Broadway finally was accomplished in 1939 with *The Philadelphia Story.* Then she went back in 1942 with a milder hit, *Without Love,* which she subsequently filmed with Spencer Tracy in 1945.

She then appeared as Rosalind in the 1950 Theatre Guild production of *As You Like It.* A lovely production, it had a successful Broadway run followed by an extended cross-country tour.

Left and top right, opposite, from *The Lake*
Bottom opposite, from *Jane Eyre*
This page, from *As You Like It*

The following year she opened in London in Shaw's *The Millionairess*. W. A. Darlington of the London *Daily Telegraph* wrote, "Nobody else that I can remember has opened in a play for which hardly any critic has a good word and by sheer personal vitality has bludgeoned her way to success."

After closing in London in September, the play came to Broadway on October 10, 1951, at the Shubert Theater for a two-week engagement. *Cue*'s review said, "Of course Miss Hepburn overacts. Of course, as you have undoubtedly heard, *The Millionairess* is a second-rate Shaw. But a dynamic actress and second-rate Shaw, assisted by good direction and cast, give a most provocative and interesting theatrical evening."

The set of portraits here and on the following pages shows the Hepburn of the late 30's. Her screen face had dispensed with some of the earlier exaggerations she had tested and, by then, had settled into the look seen here. She left Hollywood to return to the stage for *The Philadelphia Story* and when she returned to films in 1940 there was a further refinement, the M-G-M look.

In 1940, Hepburn returned to Hollywood, which she had left two years earlier with her career up in the air, to film an artful, delightful version of *The Philadelphia Story*. It was a triumph for all concerned: the picture grossed $549,000 at New York's Radio City Music Hall in the first six-week engagement. With this major achievement, Kate began a new decade with a long-term M-G-M contract and the satisfaction of being with Hollywood's major studio.

The first of Cary Grant's four films with Hepburn was *Sylvia Scarlett*, which gave new impetus to his career. His performance as a Cockney scoundrel lifted him out of the leading-man class and helped turn him into the major star he soon became.

Sylvia Scarlett, 1936 (top left). *Bringing Up Baby*, 1938 (bottom left). In 1940, Hepburn and Grant were reunited in *The Philadelphia Story* (top right).

In 1940, Hepburn was painted by artist James Chapin, who said, "The natural look of the American woman is epitomized by Katharine Hepburn."

She is seen here with McClelland Barclay, posing for a painting for the League Against Intolerance.

Woman of the Year

Keeper of the Flame

Sea of Grass

When M-G-M cast Tracy and Hepburn together in *Woman of the Year,* it brought together one of the most winning and durable duos in film history. That studio was extremely successful with its teams, starting with Garbo and Gilbert in the 20's and continuing with Crawford and Gable, MacDonald and Eddy, Garson and Pidgeon and, of course, Loy and Powell, who made an unprecedented thirteen films together.

The combination of Tracy and Hepburn was particularly irresistible to the public and critics alike. They liked their alchemy together; she was intellectual, eager and idealistic; he was down-to-earth, humorous and tolerant. Together, they made nine films: *Woman of the Year, Keeper of the Flame* (*Time* said, "For Hepburn and Tracy, it was a high point of significant failure"), *Without Love, State of the Union, Sea of Grass* (left), *Adam's Rib, Pat and Mike, The Desk Set,* and Tracy's final film, *Guess Who's Coming to Dinner?*

Here is the striking and inimitable Hepburn profile as seen over a period of thirty-six years, from her first film in 1932 to 1968.

HAIR STYLES

One of Hepburn's most striking roles was in *Dragon Seed* (1944, above), the film version of Pearl Buck's novel about China during the revolution. As Jade, Hepburn played an idealistic woman who longed for book knowledge but at the same time was realistic about life in the new China. An expensive attempt to duplicate the earlier success of Buck's *The Good Earth, Dragon Seed* had a heterogeneous cast that included Akim Tamiroff, Turhan Bey, Walter Huston, Agnes Moorehead, J. Carroll Naish, Benson Fong, Philip Ahn and Hurd Hatfield.

Throughout her career, Kate has been chided and rebuked for too many cloying, artificial mannerisms. Her style is still not entirely free of some—the tremulous catch in the voice, the too girlish head-twisting laugh, the fluttering hands, those soulful expressions—especially the tearful eyes bravely brimming over.

"When people ask me why I cry such a lot in pictures, I say mysteriously, 'Canal in Venice.'"

While filming *Summertime,* she had to fall into the canal in one sequence: "The water was a sewer, filthy, brackish. When I got out, my eyes were running and they've been running ever since. I have the most ghastly infection: I'll never lose it till the day I die."

When admirers and critics complain of aggravating mannerisms, it must be acknowledged that all great stars—male and female, stage and movie—have their fair share of them. Just think of the Barrymores, Helen Hayes, George Arliss, Cornell, Bankhead, Garbo, Wallace Beery, Davis et al. Annoying though these traits can be at times, they are part of the total personality, contributing to that *whole* which the public accepts, pays to see and gets to like.

Although she has had many illustrious male co-stars including Tracy, Barrymore, Boyer, March, Bogart, Olivier and Wayne, Hepburn has only rarely co-starred with another woman. In 1937 she and Ginger Rogers were the stars of *Stage Door* (they're seen here on the set), and in 1959 she shared billing with Elizabeth Taylor in *Suddenly, Last Summer.*

The late Joan Crawford spoke to me several times of her longing to make a film with Hepburn and, had the right property been found, what a fascinating team they would have made! At this writing, Hepburn is announced for a picture with Bette Davis. They should be an explosive combination: the two most opinionated women in films together. Will any screen be big enough to hold two such colossal film legends?

The metamorphic face of Hepburn is vividly illustrated in this melange of pictures that range from childhood to maturity. They begin with a teen-age Hepburn and continue through the peak years at RKO and M-G-M to such relatively recent films as *Suddenly, Last Summer,* and *Long Day's Journey into Night*.

CO-STARS AND LEADING MEN

John Barrymore was the star of Hepburn's first film, *A Bill of Divorcement,* in 1932 (right), but it was the only picture during her long career in which she was not starred. Seen here are some of the many co-stars from her forty-five years of movie making:

John Beal, *The Little Minister,* 1934 (bottom right)
Fred MacMurray, *Alice Adams,* 1935 (bottom left)
Charles Boyer, *Break of Hearts,* 1935 (below)
Herbert Marshall, *A Woman Rebels,* 1936 (top left, opposite)
Burt Lancaster, *The Rainmaker,* 1956 (top right, opposite)
Humphrey Bogart, *The African Queen,* 1961 (bottom, opposite)

Elsewhere in this chapter are scenes with Spencer Tracy, Cary Grant, Fredric March, Brian Aherne, Douglas Fairbanks, Jr., Adolphe Menjou and Franchot Tone.

FASHION

During the 30's and 40's Hepburn was an outstanding clothes influence and style setter. Women admired her cool elegance and ability to look comfortable and "right" in all kinds of clothes. At RKO (1932–38) Howard Greer, Muriel King and, principally, Walter Plunkett, designed her clothes. Kalloch was the designer for *Holiday*, her one film at Columbia. In 1940, when she went to M-G-M, Adrian did the clothes for her first three films at that studio, and then Irene and Walter Plunkett took over. Dressed by these outstanding couturiers, Hepburn's style and clothes flair had a considerable impact on the look of women.

In the past few decades her films have used the designing talents of Edith Head, Charles LeMaire, Norman Hartnell, Motley, Jean Louis, Margaret Furse and Rosine Delamore.

In the early 30's, along with Dietrich and Garbo, she was a forerunner with the slacks and pants the three put on the fashion map. Recently Hepburn reminisced, "Styles and personalities change. Both Marlene and I wore pants, and she wore a tuxedo and silk hat to a night club. I adored that! Marlene is a wonderful show creature. Unique! She has her own personality."

Hepburn was criticized for wearing overalls and pants and for "dressing sloppily" in her early Hollywood days. It was the era when a star was expected to be a fashion plate on all occasions. A fellow actor who had known her previously defended her. "As for wearing overalls to the studio to get publicity, that's unfair and silly. They are strictly on the level, not an affectation. She wore them daily around the company at Ivoryton."

Today, of course, the young dress mostly in slacks, pants and overalls. They *are* the fashion.

For several decades now, in her private life, Hepburn has worn what she speaks of as her "Civil War veteran's rags." Off screen, wearing no makeup, her hair "à la concierge," in old clothes and shoes, she still is no less imposing than if she were in full costume as Mary Queen of Scots or Eleanor of Aquitaine.

She wears the pants "to protect my legs"; the heavy shoes because "I'm outdoors a lot tramping in the hills with the dog"; a fatigue jacket—"My brother left it behind one day on a visit and I've worn it ever since. If it's cold, I wear a sweater beneath it"—topped always with the same cap. "I found it in Germany and I've had it copied over and over again." Except for an occasional evening out, usually at the theater, which brings forth a rarely seen dress, she wears nothing else but a variation of this outfit.

In the 30's, Hepburn was considered the ideal American girl, one with terrific fashion flair.

Bernard Newman did her clothes for *Break of Hearts,* probably the most glamorous, even theatrical, clothes she ever wore in a film.

Designer Muriel King, herself a vivid young American, was brought to Hollywood in the 30's to do clothes for two Hepburn films, *Sylvia Scarlett* and *Stage Door.* At that time she said, "Katharine Hepburn is a girl who could not look ordinary. She knows too well what she wants in clothes, and what goes with her personality. She can make a fashion, but she cannot follow one."

For *Bringing Up Baby,* her clothes were designed by Howard Greer. He had come to prominence while at Paramount and, by 1938, was a private Hollywood designer, admired for his off-screen clothes for many top stars including Garbo and Crawford. Hepburn's clothes for *Baby* have a freshness that's due partly to that off-screen look and partly to her own fresh-air personality.

Hepburn had so much distinction, such good bones and such an excellent carriage that her screen wardrobe required a similar distinction. Her personality was far too definite to fit into just any clothes. When she was younger, she felt that her neck was too long and liked to cover it with scarves and wear dresses with high necklines. She still does. "I'm not really vain, but I don't think people want to see the wrinkles on my neck; they're quite unattractive."

For *The Philadelphia Story,* Adrian created a wide-belt look that carried through all her costumes for the film. It was a trick that Hepburn repeated with the stand-up collars in *Desk Set* many years later. When something looked well and worked for her, she stuck with it.

"I'm a mixture of stock—Scottish, Welsh, Bostonish, Virginian and New England. I'm like all New Englanders, I drive a hard bargain. Fair? Don't count on it."

"I didn't get the Oscars for talent, you know. They were for years of good behavior."

"Two of the greatest assets for an actress are love and pain. She must have plenty of both in her life."

HANDS

Hepburn's dramatic use of her hands was an asset not only to her performances but also to her photographic sessions. The last photographs bring to mind Donald Ogden Stewart's observation, "St. Peter wouldn't dare argue with her at the gates of heaven."

RECENT DECADES

In the 60's her film career was brilliantly redefined with outstanding performances in *Long Day's Journey into Night, Guess Who's Coming to Dinner?* and *The Lion in Winter.* After working with her, Sidney Poitier said, "The lady is the most disciplined actress I've ever seen. Would that the stuff she's made of—the stamina, the femininity—were copiable. We could use a lot more of that in acting—and in the world."

Her aristocratic demeanor, dictatorial manner and imperious behavior caused someone (George Cukor?) to dub her "Katharine of Arrogance." She is aware of her ability to mutually attract and still put-off others. She acknowledges, "I'm a madly irritating person. And I've irritated people for years. Anything definite is irritating—and stimulative."

Long Day's Journey into Night, 1962

Song of Love, 1947

The Lion in Winter, 1968 (top left). *The Madwoma[n] of Chaillot*, 1969, which reunited Hepburn wit[h] Charles Boyer [*Break of Hearts*] and Paul Henrei[d] [*Song of Love*] (top right).
Guess Who's Coming to Dinner?, 1967 (bottom left[).] *Love Among the Ruins*, 1975 (the television fil[m] with Laurence Olivier (bottom right). *The Troja[n] Women* (opposite).

RÉSUMÉ

THARINE HEPBURN · Metro Goldwyn Mayer

When she played Gabrielle Chanel in *Coco,* it was noted that there were strong resemblances; each woman was a heady mixture of femininity and independence, well known for her inexhaustible vitality. And both responded belligerently to challenges.

When she met Chanel, Hepburn says, "She looked me up—but she didn't bother to look me down."

In his New York *Times* review of *Coco,* critic Clive Barnes said of Hepburn, "They say some beauty is ageless. Yours is timeless."

With each new venture, Hepburn predictably takes over as Miss Know-it-all. "I just want to make one little suggestion," she'll begin. But the "suggestions" never cease until the picture or the play is finished—and sometimes not even then. When she made *Guess Who's Coming to Dinner?* she announced at the beginning of the film, "In case my niece [Katharine Houghton, daughter of her youngest sister, Mrs. Ellsworth Grant of Hartford] drops dead of excitement, I'm here and I know all her lines, too!" As she poked into every cluster of activity, director Stanley Kramer finally complained, "She's into everything—with comments!" He said, "Kate, I'll give you the whole picture. You take over."

"Now, now, Stanley," she replied, "let's not lose our equilibrium."

During the production of *Coco* she so exasperated producer-lyricist Alan Jay Lerner that he cried out, "Spencer Tracy isn't dead—he's hiding!"

Director George Cukor has always been particularly adept at handling her. While filming *Keeper of the Flame,* she interrupted a fire scene to protest, "I don't think people would have to be told about a fire. They would smell the smoke!"

Cukor coolly replied, "But the screen audience can't! It must be wonderful to know all about everything, Kate—acting, writing, directing. And fires, too." Everyone laughed and work resumed.

Cukor once said, "We have always gotten along in complete harmony, I believe, because she thinks she handles me more than I handle her, putting up with more vagaries and nonsense from me than I do from her. Whatever the basis on which we work, it has always been solid and satisfactory to a huge degree."

Recently, Hepburn said what can serve as a fitting finale about herself: "I'm not as sure about everything as I seem but I *am* sure about one thing—I'm a professional actress." And of her future, "I only want to go on being a star: it's all I know how to be!"

May she, Bette Davis, Myrna Loy and Dolores Del Rio so continue!